THE POWER OF THE PADDLE

D1581248

ONE MAN'S MISSION TO INSPIRE HOPE
THROUGH THE SPIRIT OF ADVENTURE

THE
POWER
OF THE
PADDLE

JORDAN WYLIE

\Bb\
Biteback Publishing

First published in Great Britain in 2021 by
Biteback Publishing Ltd, London
Copyright © Jordan Wylie 2021

ISBN 978-1-78590-725-8

10 9 8 7 6 5 4 3 2 1

A CIP catalogue record for this book is available from the British Library.

Set in Minion Pro and Knockout

Printed and bound in Great Britain by
CPI Group (UK) Ltd, Croydon CR0 4YY

MIX
Paper from
responsible sources
FSC
www.fsc.org
FSC® C020471

In memory of Jordan Banks (2011–21), from my home town
of Blackpool. In nine short years, he showed us how
to live a whole life.

CONTENTS

ACKNOWLEDGEMENTS

I would like to say a huge thank you to the following people, who have my most sincere appreciation, my deepest gratitude and my utmost respect.

Firstly, to James Dodds and the team at the Eton Harris Group. Your friendship, kindness and unwavering support have allowed me to pursue a lifelong dream of becoming a full-time adventurer while having a positive impact on other people's lives, particularly the next generation – a huge thank you from the bottom of my heart.

To each and every person who has donated to the charities I am proud to represent, or who has supported me in any way at all, whether it was with a hot meal, a warm shower or a smiling face on the beach to welcome me after a long, tough day on the high seas. It is your incredible support that has allowed us to inspire hope for children who would otherwise most likely never have gained access to the education or opportunities we have provided. It has been one huge team effort, and all of you have been integral team members through the past few years. I hope I did you proud.

To all my teammates who were alongside me on the various adventures illustrated in this book. I have always believed that the best journeys in life are those where you are surrounded by the best people. We started these adventures as complete strangers but have finished like a family: thank you for your commitment, your belief in the mission and your spirit of endeavour to never give up, even on the occasions when I felt like I wanted to!

To James Wilkes of Gray Page and Angela and Sarah of Angel Call Handling, for believing in me and my seemingly crazy ambitious endeavours. Without your support, many of these adventures would never have materialised from a concept to a reality; I will never forget your kindness and what you enabled me to do.

To everyone at my publisher, Biteback Publishing, who have yet again given me the opportunity to tell my story to the world, thank you for your patience, for your hard work and for making the whole process an enjoyable experience: managing director James Stephens, editorial director Olivia Beattie, graphic designer Namkwan Cho and editor Lucy Stewardson.

To Ellie Osborne, for a great cover shot and for her enthusiasm and support for a complete stranger, thank you so

ACKNOWLEDGEMENTS

much. To Alice Gadney at Silver7 Mapping, the finest cartographer I have ever had the pleasure of working with, for the incredible maps at the start of this book.

To all the amazing children, Army Cadets and aspiring adventurers out there who sent me messages of support, fundraised or helped me to spread awareness throughout my expeditions: keep following your dreams and never stop believing.

To my family and friends and to my beautiful daughter Evie – you are reason I get up in the morning and try to lead by example in everything I do. I love you more than life itself.

To my good friend Alan Clark, who once again has helped me process my thoughts and feelings and turn them into a coherent story to share with you all. Without his support, professional approach and wealth of experience, this book would simply not have been possible.

Finally, to all the children of the Horn of Africa, who without knowing it gave me a purpose and passion in my life that I have never experienced before. I wish you all a lifetime of health, happiness and love in a safe and secure environment. Dream big always, and be relentless in pursuit of whatever sets your soul alive…

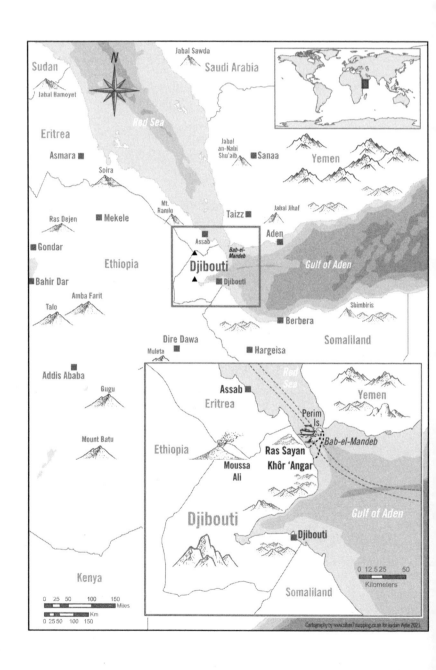

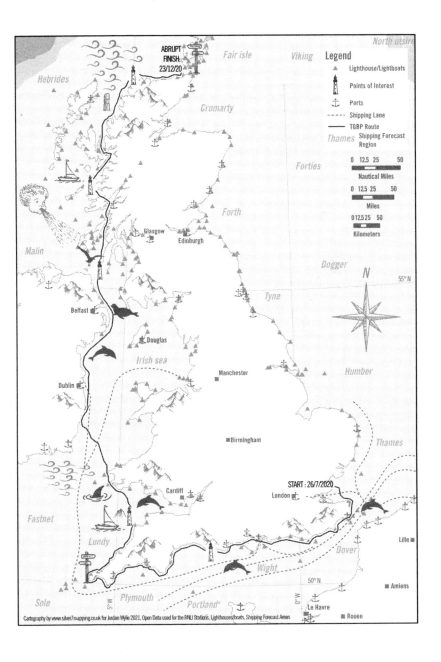

FOREWORD
BY BRENDON PRINCE

*Brendon Prince and me: two men who have been on a mission
to inspire others for many years.* © Harry Thompson

My life changed six years ago. As an off-duty beach lifeguard, I tried to rescue three people from drowning on
the north Cornish coast. All three souls perished. Since that
dark day, I have dedicated my life to educating children and

young people around the world on the importance of water safety.

As an experienced paddleboarder myself, I was excited and awed to hear about Jordan Wylie's attempt to circumnavigate Great Britain during the first bleak year of the Covid pandemic. I was even more impressed to discover his reason for doing so: to inspire hope through education for children in conflict zones and to build a school in Africa. Here, I decided, was a man after my own heart. A guy who wanted to make a difference, just as I did myself.

I hadn't met Jordan back then, but I knew of his growing reputation as an adventurer who had already done some amazing things. I felt a huge amount of respect for his courage in taking on what I knew would be an incredible feat of endurance, especially in facing the wild west coast of Scotland in winter.

As he had next to no experience of stand-up paddleboarding, I worried Jordan knew very little of what lay ahead. But what he achieved during the unchartered circumstances of the pandemic was something quite remarkable and, in its way, much bigger than any world record. In perilous conditions, he'd also done it safely and with respect for the water.

Inspired by Jordan – and once restrictions were lifted – I decided to attempt the same journey myself in aid of raising awareness of water safety on our seas, lakes and rivers.

With the generosity typical of him, Jordan gave me all the support and guidance I could have wished for. He is an absolute gentleman, a trailblazer for others and a real force for good in this complex world we live in. I salute him and the extraordinary story he tells in this book.

Brendon Prince
SUP world record holder and founder of Above Water
November 2021

CHAPTER I

IBRAHIM

His name was Ibrahim. He was about five years old and the thing he wanted most in the world was to go to school – but that was impossible because there wasn't one for him to go to. Born in war-torn Somalia, he was now a refugee in a neighbouring country. His mother and father were both dead, though mercifully he had two older sisters, so unlike thousands of other refugee kids he wasn't entirely alone in the world.

In happier times, back on the outskirts of Mogadishu, the Somali capital, Ibrahim's sisters had been able to begin a rudimentary education, and they had filled their little brother's imagination with stories of school and what great fun it was. But the terrible conflicts that had shattered Somalia for decades had caused many of its essential structures to buckle and then collapse. For its government, providing for the most basic human needs of its people was challenging enough and for many children in its worst-affected areas, education had become a distant memory. So now, in late 2018, Ibrahim and his sisters were living in an orphanage in an isolated village in the former French colony of Djibouti, a small but much more stable country on the Horn of Africa. At least there they were relatively safe and had food, water and shelter. And the orphanage was a better billet than an old mud hut in the village, where ten or fifteen children would often be crammed in under the care of local tribal elders. Yet for all of them, it was more like an existence than a life.

So, it was unlikely that Ibrahim would ever have decent shoes, a brand-new uniform or a nice leather satchel. There would be no case of pens and pencils, no ruler or calculator. Nor of course would there ever be any fond mother or father, lumps in their throats, waving him off on that red-letter day when he would take his first major step out into the world. None of the things that children in prosperous countries take for granted would be coming his way.

But little Ibrahim, and thousands of kids like him, still somehow clung to that dream. If you'd asked them why, they probably couldn't have told you very clearly. They might just have replied that school would be better than hanging around the orphanage with nothing much to do. It's not likely they'd have answered that education is the only key to some sort of future, to give you the gifts you need to take advantage of the better times that must surely come one day, somewhere over the rainbow. But even if they'd never articulated that, they still seemed instinctively to know it. And that's why, under the humble roof they now called home, kids like Ibrahim hungered for education.

It was in late 2018 that I first met Ibrahim at the orphanage near the village of As Eyla, a good few hours inland from the Djibouti capital. Despite everything he'd been through, he had that resilience which children often possess and was a happy little guy with a huge grin. He seemed to take a shine to me and stuck to me like glue as I went around on my tour. His only English word was 'football', and he kept pointing at the bright tangerine shirt which celebrated my beloved Blackpool FC. Through an interpreter, we had a long chat, and that was when he told me about that yearning to go to school. One day, he said, he'd really like to be a teacher, so he could help other kids like himself and maybe even go back to Somalia to help the other children. Despite the trauma of having lost his parents and his home, this little guy's desire to make a difference in the world was already powerful. It was humbling stuff.

As I listened to him chatter, I felt the usual flush of guilt run through me. Like almost every kid in the United Kingdom and in the other peaceful countries of the West, I had never even thought to appreciate my education. It had been handed to me on a plate and I'd turned up my nose at it. I bloody hated school. I was one of those boys who stared out of the window, gazing wistfully at the football pitch or checking the clock on the classroom wall as its hands crawled round the dial. Every minute an hour, every hour a lifetime, while the teacher droned on about the Spanish Armada or the Battle of Waterloo, about parallelograms or the geology of the Pennines. I didn't give a toss about any of it. I simply wasn't academic. Nothing morally wrong with that of course; plenty of high achievers in later life have had the same issue, but it's a disadvantage nonetheless. Like a lot of similar children, I tried to compensate for my inadequacies by becoming the class clown. Always good for a laugh. Taking the mick out of everything. Not exactly disruptive but no doubt a pain in the backside for the teachers and an irritation to those children who really did want to learn.

I was brought up on a council estate in Blackpool, which then as now was one of the most deprived towns in Britain. Wherever I travel in the world, Blackpool will always be my home. I'm proud of my town and its people; we have a community spirit that can't be found anywhere else in the world. But behind the tawdry glitter of the prom and its famous illuminations, many people led difficult lives stuck in dead-end jobs, only just making ends meet and blowing what little they had down the pub or social club on a Friday night.

Quite a few young people, boys like me who had stared out of the classroom window, had gone badly off the rails and ended up in trouble, or even becoming guests of Her Majesty in Strangeways Prison. As a wild teenager, I'd once spent a few hours in a cell myself, when a policeman had caught me peeing in a local park after a few drinks of some cheap cider, and I'd given him a bit too much lip in return. Luckily, I'd been blessed with two loving parents, who gave me some tough love, always believed in me and kept me on the straight and narrow. Eventually, like my dad, I went into the military, and that sorted me out good and proper. As with so many lads from humble backgrounds, the army was the making of me, teaching me discipline and the values I needed to eventually make something of my life. In the army, I discovered for the first time that there were things I actually *wanted* to learn, and so I did. But there's no denying that I threw away my formal education and left school with two pretty lousy GCSEs that were of sod all use to anyone.

And then, all these years later, here was little Ibrahim with his big grin and his shining, hopeful eyes, telling me how much he longed to go to school. Every morning in Blackpool, I was dragged kicking and screaming towards the transformative gift of education; Ibrahim would have run towards it, his arms open wide. Shame on me.

It was the military that first took me to this troubled part of the world, where kids like Ibrahim struggled to survive. I had served in the King's Royal Hussars in both Iraq and Northern Ireland, seen some awful things, had some close shaves and, tragically, lost a few wonderful and inspiring mates. Eventually, though, a back injury derailed my military career and I became a maritime security guard, protecting huge oil tankers and container ships off the Horn of Africa from the terrible scourge of violent piracy that mushroomed in these waters during the first and second decades of the twenty-first century. And despite the fact that the Middle East had now become synonymous with conflict and terrorism, I'd come to love it. Despite its undoubted dangers, especially for Westerners like me, I was seduced both by the stunning beauty of the landscapes and by the warmth, friendliness and amazing courage of the ordinary people I came across.

But it was always the kids who really got to me. At the time of writing, in summer 2021, UNICEF estimates that there are 11 million children currently at risk of hunger, disease and death due to the war in Yemen. The Red Cross suggests that several million people have been already displaced, seeking refuge from that conflict and from the never-ending strife in the other troubled lands around the Horn of Africa. And now, on top of it all, there is Covid. It is, in short, the perfect storm. The world's charities are doing their bit of course, admirably and against spectacular odds, but it is easy to see the cup not just as half-empty but as almost totally drained.

Undoubtedly, this corner of the globe is now one of the worst places for a child to be born; their prospects are blighted from the start. But then you clock the face of little Ibrahim with his mile-wide grin and his hopes for the future, and your despair seems like an unforgivable indulgence, a coward's response. Surely something can be done – must be done. And so, I asked myself, what could I do? Obviously, like anyone else, I could donate money to the charities. Obviously too, I could raise some money myself, as I'd recently done by running through Iraq, Afghanistan and Somalia on a previous adventure.

But now, I decided, there needed to be something more. This time, I'd do something a bit more special, a bit more personal. And then the thought flew into my mind, nested there and wouldn't budge. It was Ibrahim's dream to go to a school that didn't exist. OK then. I was going to build it.

CHAPTER 2

'I'VE HEARD IT ALL BEFORE, MR WYLIE'

It was fairly obvious what he thought of me. He didn't say it, but it was pretty clear from his eyes as he looked me up and down. He himself was immaculately dressed in suit and tie, and most people who entered his large, imposing office would have made the effort to be equally smart. But here I was, a guy he had never heard of, a guy who looked, I had to admit, like a bit of a scumbag. Ripped T-shirt, shorts, flip-flops, a dark shadow of stubble. It just wasn't a good look for an important meeting with the Minister of Education for the Republic of Djibouti, the man whose agreement and support I would need if I was going to keep the promise I had made to Ibrahim and build his school.

But I'd not come to Djibouti expecting to have a high-powered meeting with a top government official. I'd travelled out on a recce for my next extreme adventure, which was to be the first person to row across the dangerous Bab el-Mandeb Strait between Africa and Arabia. This world-record attempt was scheduled for about a year later, in October 2019, but there was lots of pre-planning to sort out, getting the necessary permissions to make the trip and solving the logistics of transporting a specially designed boat out from the UK. As usual in this part of the world, tasks that would have been fairly straightforward in Britain were much more problematic. Dealing with it all from my front room in Andover, Hampshire, wasn't really a viable option, so here I was.

Most people in the UK, even well-educated ones, have never even heard of Djibouti. Roughly the size of Wales, it's a small country by African standards but nowadays it's a very important place. This importance lies in two things: first, its strategic position on the Gulf of Aden at the gateway between the Red Sea (and the Suez Canal) and the Indian Ocean. This prime location is the reason for its other benefit – there are foreign military bases all over it, especially belonging to China and the USA, their presences bringing to Djibouti not just a large income but also a degree of stability and security that is almost unknown in many of the surrounding dysfunctional states. That's why so many refugees flee from the trauma of their conflict zones towards Djibouti. It is a beacon of safety. A promised land where they can find some shelter from the horrors they've seen. And among them, huge numbers of children like Ibrahim and his sisters.

During my years in the maritime security industry, I spent a fair bit of time in Djibouti and made many contacts there. So, once the idea of building a school had blazed into my mind, I made a phone call to a local businessman I had worked with in the past – a man of some influence. My friend made a phone call or two in his turn, maybe pulled the odd string. At first, we were told that there was no chance the Minister of Education could see Mr Jordan Wylie (and who the hell is *he*, anyway?). So, as I was due to fly home very shortly, it was looking like a no-goer. But eventually the call came out of the blue to say that the minister had a very brief window and would be graciously pleased to receive me if I could get to his office in the next half-hour. It was a heck of a rush, hence the shorts, the flip-flops and the stubble. I normally try my best to make a great first impression, but I simply didn't have time to get changed and grab a shower and a shave, unfortunately!

But when I got to his grand office in the poshest part of Djibouti City, I soon realised that my appearance wasn't the sole drawback. The cynicism and world-weariness of the minister was going to be the greater issue.

'In this office, Mr Wylie, I've listened to many generous

offers of help and support for our country in this difficult situation,' he said with a smile and a sigh. 'But I'm afraid that they rarely come to fruition. We've been let down many times.'

'Well, I won't let you down,' I replied.

'I'm sure you wouldn't mean to, Mr Wylie, but there are many obstacles in this part of Africa which might be more challenging than you imagine.'

I assumed that he was referring to the corruption that was a plague in most of these African countries, even one as relatively peaceful as Djibouti. There was little doubt that money and supplies sent through the big charities sometimes never reached the desperate people for whom it had been so laboriously raised, ending up instead lining the pockets of dishonest officials and tribal leaders. So, I needed the minister to know that I wasn't a total innocent in this neck of the woods. I told him a little about my experiences as a soldier, about my days fighting the pirates in the Gulf and about the fundraising efforts I'd already achieved with my running expeditions in the Middle East. I emphasised too that I wasn't some big, lumbering non-governmental organisation (NGO) with overheads to pay; I was just one guy who wanted to make a difference, and this ostensible negative was in fact a positive.

The minister asked me to wait outside his office. It was a bloody long wait, maybe forty-five minutes. I began to think this was a bit rude, but I guessed he was probably making some calls and checking me out. Eventually, I flip-flopped back into his office, feeling like a naughty schoolboy summoned to the headmaster's study. Luckily, the minister had warmed up a bit by now.

'Very well, Mr Wylie,' he said. 'The government of Djibouti will give you a plot of land. You have two years to build your school. If it isn't up and running by the end of that period, we will take the land back from you and the project will be terminated. Is that agreeable to you?'

'That's fine by me,' I said and shook his hand.

I looked the guy straight in the eye to show him that I meant what I said. In those eyes, however, the hint of cynicism still lingered. Despite his offer, I still sensed that his hopes weren't high. I made a little vow to myself that the next time I entered this office, the man in the smart suit would shake my hand in a totally different way, that it would be a shake of congratulations and that the school would now be a thing not just of dreams and promises but of bricks and mortar. I also vowed that the next time I'd be dressed like a male model out of *GQ* magazine.

Over the next few weeks, the details would be thrashed out. I'd be offered three potential sites for the school. One of them was at As Eyla, very near to where I'd first met Ibrahim, so that's the one I went for. The Djibouti government would help me appoint a project manager to oversee the whole operation and hire the architects, the construction companies, their labourers and so on. Once the actual building was completed, the government would take it over and run it, pay the teachers and provide all the necessary equipment. At As Eyla, it was calculated that the need was for a primary school to educate around 250 children aged four to seven, made up of refugees and orphans from the various regional conflicts as well as local Djibouti kids with no previous access to learning. The estimated price tag was around $350,000. All I had to do was find the money.

Bloody hell. How was I going to do that? It was clearly the biggest thing I'd ever taken on, though I had no idea quite how enormous it would turn out to be. Thank Christ for that. If I had, I might have run for the hills and justified all the minister's worst fears. But I also knew in my heart that it was the most important goal on which I'd ever set my sights. Above all, I knew that to raise the dosh, to get people's attention in a world crammed with worthy causes, I'd have to do something seriously amazing that would get plenty of media interest, attract sponsorship and make people put their hands in their pockets. As my plane took off from Djibouti, I didn't yet have a clue what that might be. I only knew that somewhere way down there on the arid plains were a couple of hundred kids whose lives I might be able to change for the better. And there was no way I was going to flunk it and fail them. No way.

For the next year or so, whenever things got tough, miserable and seemingly hopeless (and they sure would), I'd try to keep those 250 faces at the front of my mind. Young kids who'd already been through hell but who still loved to laugh and to kick a football around on a dusty scrap of African earth. At those moments, I'd say to myself, come on Jordan. Get your act together. You can do this. Stay in the game.

CHAPTER 3

KICKING THE BLACK DOG

Flashback a few years from that office in Djibouti, and there I was, glass in hand, chatting to Her Majesty the Queen at Windsor Castle – as one does.

In the gilded splendour of her vast front room, we were having a natter about racehorses, which, as everyone knows, is HMQ's specialist subject. It was a long natter too, a good twenty minutes or so, to the slight irritation of some of her officials and the other guests. The way these gigs work, twenty minutes equated to about a fortnight. But once HMQ gets going about horseflesh, there's no shutting her up. She was absolutely lovely, and I was of course entranced. Not just by my awesome hostess but by our spectacular surroundings. How did I, a boy from Blackpool who had left school with virtually nothing, find himself under the chandeliers having a conflab with the direct descendant of William the Conqueror (1066 and all that)?

The answer, indirectly, was money. By this point in my life, I was flush enough – and flash enough – to be part-owner of a beautiful racehorse. An officer under whom I'd served in the King's Royal Hussars, and who had subsequently become a great friend, had turned himself into a big-league racehorse trainer and invited me to purchase a new prospect that had just arrived at the stables in Lambourn, Berkshire. Sadly, the animal in question was never destined to be Red Rum and it didn't end up being one of my best investments, but we had some great fun and brilliant days out. But every year at the Grand Military Gold Cup at Sandown Park, the owners of the competing horses (even the losers) are invited for drinkies and canapés up at the castle. And that's how the road on which I'd found myself in life had led me to this glittering palace, necking the champers and nibbling the posh people's version of Twiglets.

The reason I'm telling you this is that I'd increasingly come to question whether or not that glitzy, ritzy road was the one I ought to have been on in the first place. Eventually, I would decide that it wasn't and change my direction, swapping the majestic road to Windsor with the dirty, dusty road to Ibrahim's village in Djibouti. But switching tracks had been a long, hard process; a process which, at one dreadful moment, had almost ended my life. In my last book, *Running For My Life*, I told the tale of this personal journey at some length, so I want to keep it short here. But I'd like you to understand how, and more importantly *why*, that journey needed to happen.

At the time of mixing it up with the rich and famous from around the world, I was leading what a lot of folk would consider a glamorous life. I was still based in an ordinary house in Hampshire with my partner Laura and our young daughter Evie. Sometimes, I'd still drive down to Tesco to do the shopping or have a drink down the local pub with my mates. But a lot of the time, I worked away from that ordinary, grounded base and inhabited a very different world, which centred around London and international travel. A world of smart offices, smart hotels, smart suits and some very smart people. It was a seductive world and I'd been seduced.

This degree of absence from home had been going on for a long time. Laura had got used to it since my time in the armed services. Then, after ten years in the military, I had like many other former soldiers joined the 'Gold Rush' into the maritime security business. This new Klondike had come about because of the sudden insurgency of pirates, mostly Somali, in the war-torn waters off the Horn of Africa and in the Indian Ocean. Suddenly, one of the world's most vital trade routes was in real jeopardy, with the massive oil tankers and container ships now at serious risk of hijacking by three or four scruffy guys in a skiff armed with AK-47s, and the ship's crews being held for extortionate ransoms. Organised crime had quickly moved in and horror stories of what captured crews had suffered began to mount up. One of the most notorious cases was dramatised in the film *Captain Phillips*, starring Tom Hanks – a Hollywood film that I had the great privilege of working on in an advisory role.

Naturally, the global shipping industry fought back, and large numbers of security guards, mostly ex-military, were offered eye-watering sums to 'ride shotgun' aboard these huge vessels, protecting the ships with physical measures, training their crews in what to do in the event of a pirate attack and being ready to repel boarders with bullets if it should come to that. Stints on the ships could last for several weeks or longer, and a string of consecutive assignments could mean I wouldn't get home for a couple of months. It wasn't good for being somebody's partner or somebody's father. But for the first time in my life I had big bucks in the bank. I could buy nice things, which I hoped would compensate for my absences. I also used the long spells at sea to give myself the education I'd so carelessly tossed aside back in Blackpool. While many of my mates spent their free time in their cabins watching dodgy DVDs, I started studying for qualifications in maritime security and related issues. The other guys teased me a bit, but I didn't care. Somewhere inside me was a growing and ever more compulsive need to build up some kind of lasting career that would not only allow my family a high standard of living but would also give me a real sense of purpose and achievement. I had seen too many former soldiers struggling to cope in 'Civvy Street' like fish out of water. It wasn't a pretty sight, and I was determined that it wasn't going to happen to me.

And my strategy worked. In time, I got myself a string of degrees in maritime security and risk management: foundation, undergraduate and post-graduate. The industry was still a fairly small world, and my reputation gradually grew, not just as an experienced, cool-headed operator with a gun but as a go-to expert on the theory and practice of maritime security. By the mid-2010s the peak years of Somali piracy had passed, but it had been a massive wake-up call for the shipping companies. Few large vessels now risked the Horn of Africa without strong security. And there was a new threat too, arguably greater than the pirates had ever been: cyber security. This was the new bogeyman that disturbed the dreams not just of the shipping business but of commercial enterprises and governments all over the world. So, I set myself to learn as much as I could about this latest phenomenon too, getting in on the ground floor of what was clearly going to be a money-spinner for a lot of people. Why shouldn't I be one?

In an attempt to spend more time with my partner and my daughter, I gradually wound down my trips on ships and through my connections in the industry was offered a land-based job with an international maritime security company. A company for which, still in my early thirties, I was to become managing director. Big job, big bucks, big thrill. We had smart Mayfair offices, and when I had to stay over in London I was billeted in the ultra-chic hotel along the street. I'd get invited to business dinners and awards evenings, wearing black tie, drinking brandy, smoking cigars and buying the back legs of that racehorse. Every five minutes I was packing a bag and jumping on a plane, usually turning left at the top of the aircraft steps. I soon got used to lots of posh hotels: marble bathrooms, azure swimming pools and white-coated waiters ready, at a wave of my hand, to refill my Diet Coke or, for all I knew, to pick my nose. More than once I suppressed the urge to send postcards to the teachers back home who had decided I was thick and going nowhere.

Of course, none of this did much to improve my domestic situation. A man with two lives in half a dozen different places; my partner was getting more, not less, fed up. Even when I was physically at home, my mind often wasn't; I was welded to my phone, totally focused on my working life. Eventually, the lolly I brought home and the way of life we could now afford no longer made up for the fact that Laura had almost become a single parent. The cracks in the house in Andover were getting wider by the week. I could only guess how long it might go on standing.

To cut the sad story short, the house eventually fell down. My partner found somebody else and I was faced with the earth-shattering prospect that my daughter, who despite my constant absences still meant more than anything to me, would soon be living under the same roof as another man. A stranger to her. A substitute father. That was the bitterest pill I could possibly swallow, even if I was largely responsible for the outcome. In fact, I refused to swallow it for many months, believing that somehow Laura and I could still make a go of things and keep our home together for the sake of Evie. But it was a fool's errand. Laura now wanted a life with somebody else and that was that. Telling Evie that her mummy and daddy were no longer going to be together was one of the worst moments of my life. I could fight the enemy in Iraq or the pirates off Somalia, but all that was child's play compared with telling my seven-year-old kid that our little family was breaking up.

The next few months were hellish. My mind was getting darker all the time, which soon fed into my body. One day, my stomach cramps and shits were so bad I was writhing on the bed and an ambulance had to be called. One of the paramedics, who had been in the military, recognised raw stress when she saw it, the body finally telling the mind it couldn't take it any more.

'Come on, Jordan, you've got to man up now,' she whispered. 'You're an ex-soldier. Get to your GP right away and sort yourself out.'

But still, I didn't. Stupid masculine pride, I guess. All that macho crap. I didn't like to admit 'failure' at anything, let alone at what is the most important aspect of all our lives: the giving and receiving of love. I still clung to the notion that somehow Laura and I could snatch some sort of victory from the jaws of defeat.

Miraculously – God knows how – I managed to keep all this stuff separate from my work and maintain a reasonable public front, but on my days off I'd slob around the house, unwashed and unshaven, drinking too much beer and watching crap TV with the curtains drawn. Once Laura and Evie moved out, I let the place go. Housework just wasn't my thing, and it wasn't long before it was hard to decide which of us looked worse: me or the house.

Though the paramedic had meant well, the point came when I could no longer simply 'sort myself out'. I was way beyond that now. Way beyond. The snowball was rolling downhill and getting ever larger. Gradually I realised that something had happened which I'd never imagined could ever affect the likes of me. Me, a big, strong guy, 6ft 2 in.,

16 stone, who'd served in several war zones, seen some pretty grim stuff and dealt with it. That 'something' of course was a serious mental health problem, ultimately diagnosed as severe anxiety and depression. But still I carried on; the work was still coming in, I still boarded aircraft to exotic destinations, I was still Jordan Wylie, professional security consultant and cock of the walk.

But then, surely as night follows day, the whole thing came to a head. The moment when I wasn't even sure I wanted to go on living. Unfortunately, that moment came in a very dangerous place indeed: ninety floors above the ground on the roof of an apartment building in Dubai. I was there on another job, sharing an apartment with a couple of business partners from whom I had somehow managed to hide my rapidly crashing mental state. But of course I couldn't hide it from myself and the bleak morning ultimately came when, spaced out, almost robotic, I slipped out of the luxurious apartment without saying goodbye to anyone and found the dank and dreary service staircase that led up to the roof. I sat there looking out over the soaring skyscrapers of the desert city; a place full of noise and vulgarity, big flash cars and people scrambling around furiously making pots of money. Dubai was the perfect symbol of the life I'd come to lead but which, in the end, had brought me to the state in which I now found myself. How ironic that I was perched on top of a ninety-storey pinnacle when my spirits were down in the darkest depths. And how easy it would be to just take a deep breath, stand up, run towards the edge of the roof and launch myself into oblivion.

Yet instead of rushing towards that fatal edge, I just sat there for hours as the fierce sun moved across the sky, thinking about my life, the people I cared for and the people I now felt I'd let down (who were usually one and the same). Of course, as any psychotherapist in the first ten minutes of their training could have worked out, the person I'd let down most was myself. Somehow, without even noticing, I'd lost touch with my core values. The values which my mum and dad had drummed into me in order to keep me safe from the mistakes so many of the kids around me had fallen into. The values which the army had drummed into me too: integrity, courage, loyalty, discipline, selfless commitment and respect for others. All these things had once been the criteria against which I'd measured myself and the goals I'd strived so hard to achieve.

But in my obsession to 'make something' of myself, I had indeed lost those values. And the person I'd 'made' I didn't really recognise and certainly didn't much like. I even realised that I no longer saw myself as what most people would call 'a good man'. How awful, how sheer bloody awful was that? As I sat on the roof, I scrolled down the texts and emails that had piled up from Laura. Legal things that needed attention but which I'd not done. Financial arrangements for Evie. All that stuff. The texts were angry, disappointed, disillusioned, most of her respect for me long since gone. Now the roof seemed to shrink, its edges creeping in towards me.

That I didn't let it come any closer was due to sheer good luck more than anything. Suddenly, up on that desolate roof under the blazing sun, my phone buzzed again. That same phone which was stuffed with so many angry messages now brought me love and support. 'Mum', it said.

'How are you? Is everything OK?' She'd known of course that things were pretty bad, though not just how ill I was becoming. But somehow, from 4,500 miles away in Blackpool, something had told her to text her boy. And so I rang her.

'What's up, Jord? You don't sound right. Are you having a tough time, love?'

And hearing my mother's voice coming to me from my old home, saying that however awful things currently were it wouldn't be the end of the world, meant that it wasn't. The woman who had given me life now unknowingly saved it. I told her a little, but not everything. A very sensible woman, she'd certainly not always taken my side during the crisis, and now she told me that I needed to let go of Laura and move on with my own life. Yet maybe she sensed something darker in my voice that day. 'Don't do anything stupid, Jord,' she said.

'Think of Evie. She needs her father. She really misses you. Come on home.'

The edge of the roof expanded away from me. How even for a second could I have thought of doing such a thing to my parents, to my ex-partner and above all to my beautiful daughter? What a dreadful legacy to leave her. I suddenly felt very selfish. Unlike my mates who had perished in Iraq and Afghanistan, I was still able to watch the sun come up in the mornings. I still had an incredible daughter. I had skills and talents and was respected in my work. I was young and hopefully had decades still in front of me which I could choose to use in any way I wanted. But first of all, I must get home. I must get help.

And so I did. At first it was a struggle. My local GP, though kind and well-meaning, insisted that my severe depression and chronic anxiety was actually post-traumatic stress disorder (PTSD), an illness which affects people in all walks of life but particularly in the military. My current mental health, he thought, was simply the long-delayed aftershocks of my tours in Iraq; the terrible things I'd seen and the losses I'd suffered. But I knew in my gut it wasn't that. PTSD is an odd condition; some people can suffer badly after relatively mild traumas, while others can witness truly devastating things yet not be afflicted to any serious degree. I was convinced that I was firmly in the latter group and that the simple core reason for my dire state was the disintegration of my family. And the person to blame for that was me and nobody else.

Eventually, though, I managed to be believed and like a good boy I started to take the anti-depressants, those magic bullets which slowly got me back onto a reasonably even keel. Chemically, at least. I hated having to take medication. I'd always thought popping pills was an admission of some sort of weakness or failure and was nervous too of the possibility of addiction. They took effect slowly, but I have to admit, they were like a life jacket thrown to a drowning man, keeping me afloat until I could reach dry land again. Yet though I realised I'd need to take the meds for a fair old time, I knew they weren't the sole answer. So, I tried various forms of psychotherapy, but I quickly felt it wasn't right for me and that I'd need to take this in hand myself. I'd have to make major changes to reboot myself into a man I'd be happy to face in the bathroom mirror every morning. My love for my daughter and knowing she still needed me was a major motivation spurring me on to make those changes. But I knew I'd also need to find some new direction in life that would give me back the self-respect and purpose I'd so carelessly, but devastatingly, lost. I knew that big bucks wouldn't be part of it. The days of flashy hotels, smart suits and turning left into business class were gone. There would be no more racehorses or lovely chats with the Queen at Windsor Castle. Whatever it was, I wanted it to be some sort of rebirth for Jordan Wylie – and some way to kick the black dog of depression in the balls and send it running for cover.

CHAPTER 4

ADVENTURER

The word 'adventurer' has a complex history. When I was a lad, it meant the likes of Indiana Jones in distant climes with his bullwhip and fedora, Robin Hood with his bow and arrow and Sir Francis Drake capturing gold from the Spaniards. All flashing swords and deeds of derring-do. All that *Boy's Own* stuff. But there was a definite 'bad boy' vibe too, and as we're now increasingly aware, not all these picture-book heroes were admirable – and some quite the reverse. In the early to mid-twentieth century, the word 'adventurer' seemed to go into storage for a while; men like Captain Scott and Sir Edmund Hillary, who climbed Mount Everest, were just called 'explorers' or 'pioneers'. But in the new millennium, the adventurer has come roaring back, reinvented to mean something wholly positive. This time, though, it's usually preceded by the adjective 'extreme'. Today's extreme adventurer is usually someone, male or female, who loves to take on mind-boggling challenges both physical and mental, establishing new records and pushing out the boundaries of what human beings can achieve. The new gallery includes people like my friends Nimsdai Purja and Aldo Kane and household names like Bear Grylls and many more. Their amazing feats are not just chronicled in mainstream newspapers but now take centre stage in reality TV programmes and on social media, where millions can follow their exploits at the click of a button. I never deliberately set out to join that remarkable band, but somehow, amazingly, that's what has happened. I ain't complaining.

That new direction I'd been looking for came to me fairly easily. In fact, it had been bubbling beneath my consciousness for a long time and just needed something to bring it to the surface. That something was to be my dark day of the soul on the rooftop in Dubai and my subsequent battle to get the help I needed. The new direction itself came both from my years as a soldier in war zones and from my time fighting the Somali pirates, where I'd been struck so often by how very little so many people have in this world. It was obviously easy to feel pity for the civilian casualties of conflicts; it was a lot less easy to empathise with the pirate boys in their skiffs with their AK-47s, terrorising the seas and sometimes killing people. Yet they too had usually led lives of great deprivation.

They too had once been children with dreams of some kind of better life.

All that stuff was the reason I was first drawn into visiting orphanages in some of those troubled countries. Hard to explain why. Just some general, unfocused urge to see if I could do anything to help. Many people would scoff at that notion and ask what one bloke could expect to achieve. My answer to that is: 'Bollocks.' If every well-meaning person who genuinely wants to make a difference in this world actually did something about it, the change would be massive. It doesn't matter what you do: it could be simply sending money, raising funds with an event in your workplace or maybe even sponsoring a child in a war zone. So many images of the kids I'd encountered every day as a soldier had stayed with me. Many of them lived in a brutal, frightening environment. They played in streets littered with the debris of conflict: guns, tanks, artillery shells, damaged buildings, homes half-ruined. Yet with the amazing fortitude children can have, they were nearly always smiling or laughing, interested to know who you were and where you came from. Often cheeky and out for a bit of fun. Just like myself at that age. But no doubt there were still times, when the bombs exploded and the bullets flew, when they were frightened half to death and their sleep was filled with nightmares.

But perhaps the thing which depressed me most was the lack of opportunity they had. What a bloody lousy start in life these kids were having. Even if they survived the worst of these wars, how could they ever prosper and build some sort of decent existence as adults? I remember the day I encountered a group of children in Iraq out on one of the main transit routes. One of the kids had inadvertently initiated a roadside bomb; there were casualties and losses and it was another dark day I remember so well. I was upset, angry and shocked by what I saw, and I struggled to process it for many years. 'Christ, don't these kids have a school to go to?' I'd said in frustration to our interpreter.

'Well, no, they don't actually,' he'd replied.

His answer stopped me in my tracks. It turned out the nearest school to that place was 60km away, and as most of these families were extremely poor, without transport or even their own fixed abode, sending their children there was a non-starter. These kids would simply never experience education as I'd known it. And that was the moment, processing what had just happened with those children, that I made a quiet vow to myself that one day, somehow, I'd try to help children living in these blighted places to get some kind of basic education. It might not be for very many kids, it might not be anything like the schooling I'd so carelessly undervalued, but it would be something. I remember that moment like it was yesterday. And so, when I finally started to drag my life back together, the new purpose I needed was right there before me. I just had to reach out and grasp it.

In the meantime, though, I had my own child to support and my own bills to pay, and I would only gradually be able to make the transition from one way of life to another. So I had to keep on accepting assignments as a maritime security consultant. Apart from the good money this brought in, getting out and about was better for my mental health than slobbing on the sofa in Andover and feeling sorry for myself. One of these was a gig escorting an American TV crew around the Horn of Africa as they made a documentary about piracy. It was enjoyable and interesting work, and I was flattered I'd been asked to contribute.

Then one day I was bitten by a mosquito – a daily occurrence in such places of course, but this particular little bastard was far more dangerous than most. I soon began to feel very ill indeed, throwing up every five minutes. The Americans assumed it was seasickness and enjoyed taking the piss out of me, just as I'd been doing to those among them who'd been afflicted. But I knew it wasn't that. I knew this was something else entirely and that I was getting worse by the hour. A few days later, having lost power in my legs, pouring with sweat, my muscles aching and my head pounding like a hammer, I found myself quarantined in a hospital ward in Djibouti.

Everyone was scared I'd contracted Ebola, that dreadful virus that kills many of its victims, and that I'd brought it into Djibouti. My bed was covered in a white tent and the medics treating me were protected inside kit that made it look like they were on Mars. They were really scared but not half as scared as I was, facing the possibility of dying alone far away from my family. But I was lucky. The blood tests showed it wasn't Ebola but another very nasty tropical illness called dengue fever. It was three weeks before I was well enough to fly back to the UK, still feeling like death warmed up and still chucking up every half-hour. The taxi driver friend who met me at Heathrow had to stop the cab a few times so I could be sick on the verge. 'Jord, mate, I'm taking you to hospital. You look like you've gone ten rounds with Mike Tyson,' he said.

Despite my protests, I ended up in Winchester Hospital, where the whole circus began again. They too were alarmed by the remote possibility of Ebola, so once again I was quarantined while all the tests were done a second time. Luckily, dengue fever was confirmed. Unluckily, I was still curled up in a foetal position, unable to lift my head or form a coherent sentence. It was a slow recovery and a dreadful experience. I hoped and prayed that by now that bastard mosquito had met a very unpleasant end under the heel of somebody's shoe or splattered against a wall.

As I grew stronger, I began to focus again on the new

direction I wanted to take. By chance, when passing through Ethiopia I came across a phrase written on a wall that really hit the spot. It resonated with me so strongly it has become a sort of personal philosophy and a mantra I repeat to myself and to other people as often as I can: 'Be the difference that makes a difference.' In seven words, it nailed what I wanted to do with the rest of my life.

My mind buzzed with dozens of possible ideas before it landed on the one I felt really had legs. The project would be called 'Running Dangerously', and the objective would be to run a marathon in each of the three conflict zones in which I'd either worked or served – Iraq, Afghanistan and Somalia – raising money for the major charities operating in those parts of the world. I hoped that an ex-squaddie returning to do something positive in the damaged countries where I'd been a soldier would get that attention – and it did. It's important to me to say that whatever people think about the wisdom of these wars, and specifically about Britain's involvement in them, I don't believe a single British soldier ever went without a genuine desire to do some good. They might never express that in a million years, but it's hidden underneath the usual jokes and banter and that quiet professional determination to 'get on with the job', and I have no doubt it was always there. So obviously it was depressing when your desire to protect the local population from violence and insurgency wasn't welcome and you knew that at least some of them saw you as invaders. I reckoned it would be meaningful to go back to these places where I'd maybe once been a symbol of something negative and try to become a symbol of the opposite.

In a world where so many charities are competing to raise funds, I knew I needed to do something that would push boundaries and grab the imaginations of large numbers of potential donors. Plenty of people ran marathons in exotic places, either for good causes or just to break a record as a personal athletic goal. But nobody had run long distances through all three of the most dangerous war zones in the world. Plus, my 'good cause' was surely one of the best: to improve the educational prospects of the next generations in these turbulent places, and by doing so to help bring them better times.

But I wasn't totally being Mother Teresa; I had a selfish motive too. I knew that the running would be good for me; not just because of its worthy aim but because, as every shrink will tell you, the sheer physical business of exercise is hugely beneficial to mental health. It's as if the oxygen pumping through the brain dissolves the tangled knots of tension inside your head. The issues that stress you out and lead to anxiety and depression may still be there, but somehow exercise helps you get perspective on them, helping to blow away your most negative thoughts and replace them with much more positive feelings about yourself and your future. I knew I still needed the drugs for my anxiety and depression, though I continued to be concerned about their long-term effects. I knew that the adrenaline and cortisone which flood the body during exercise could be addictive too, but that was in a good way. I'd certainly rather be hooked on a run in the park than on some chemical cosh. So I really hoped that Running Dangerously would be exactly what I needed to counteract the recent years of doom and gloom, to kick away the black dog once and for all and to really reset my life.

Happily, the sponsors rolled in, large and small. Lloyd's of London supported me in getting the vital but expensive insurance to cover me in hostile environments. Others contributed with plane tickets, running kit, satellite phones and tracking equipment and a hundred other things that are needed for a serious, well-prepared adventure. A thousand quid here, a hundred there, every little helped. And it was a massive boost to get public support from high-profile people like Dame Kelly Holmes and Sir Ranulph Fiennes, two people who have always inspired me over the years.

Of course, lots of people thought I was mad running such a risk. A former British soldier returning to these dangerous countries might well be a target for Al-Qaeda, Al-Shabaab, the Taliban or any of the other destructive fanatical sects who still hold so much sway. So there needed to be a balance between generating enough publicity to bring in the dosh but not so much that I put myself into the crosshairs of some insurgent's AK-47. The precise timings and locations needed to be kept tightly under wraps.

In the end, it wasn't some murderous zealot who was the biggest threat to Running Dangerously but an Englishman sitting in a room in Andover, who only had my best interests at heart. 'You can't be serious, Mr Wylie,' said my GP with a look of absolute horror on his face. 'You absolutely cannot do this right now. In fact, it would be downright dangerous, irresponsible and reckless. You're simply going to have to give up on this idea, however laudable it is. I'm very sorry.'

The cause of his horror was that sodding little mosquito. During the planning stages for the trip I'd still been doing some maritime security work. On a business visit to the south of France, I'd suddenly keeled over on a quayside and blacked out. A crowd had gathered, somebody had tried CPR and an air ambulance had been summoned. I had no memory of it at all – I'd fallen flat on my face and it was a surprise to see my bruised and bloody features in a mirror. Back home, all sorts of tests were done and the diagnosis made. It had been a mild epileptic seizure. What? You've got to be kidding? But there was no doubt at all. The NHS doctors were baffled as to the reason; there was no family history. Then I had another seizure, milder this time, sitting on the sofa watching TV. I started to really worry about the impact on Running Dangerously. Eventually, I took myself off to a private doctor, who scrambled around in my medical records and found the definitive answer. It turned out that a small number of people who contract dengue fever suffer a legacy of epilepsy. And I was one. Hopefully long since squashed flat, the sodding mosquito was still trying to get me from its grave.

I was, as they say, gutted. The plans for Running Dangerously were well advanced by now. The sponsors were lined up. I'd already got £25,000 of funding. The media had really woken up to the project; there had been pieces in national newspapers and magazines and loads of interviews on TV and radio already. There was just no way I could give up. It was inconceivable. Not only would I disappoint so many people, I'd disappoint myself, and the black dog would no doubt be barking at my door again. But I was wise enough to know that I had to share the doctor's judgement with my sponsors, my friends and my family and make it clear to them that there was now an extra dimension to the undoubted risks I was already running. I fully expected that the sponsors might pull out and that my family would try to persuade me to abandon the attempt. But then something great happened. The more the news got out about my epilepsy, and that I was still determined to run despite it, the more support

I got. Epilepsy Action saw me on TV and asked if I would become an ambassador for the charity. 'What you want to do is incredible,' they said. 'Having epilepsy doesn't have to ruin your life. If it's managed sensibly, there's no reason why your life should change.' Those were the words I wanted to hear. The next were even better: 'Your expedition can help others to see they can still follow their dreams and live life to the full.'

This was the rocket I needed. Now it seemed the project might do some good for a totally different group of people, quite separate from the front-line children who were its primary focus. I was more determined than ever. Yes, Mum, I would be sensible. Yes, I would take every precaution possible. But nothing would stop me. Not well-meaning doctors. Not my mental health. And certainly not a bloody mosquito.

So the final preparations were made. And boy, there were so many things to think about. Things you imagine are trivial, only to discover later that they're really important and you're forced to kick your own arse very hard indeed. Now, on every adventure I plan, I make sure I never forget that famous old military motto of the 'Seven Ps': prior preparation and planning prevents piss-poor performance.

And so Running Dangerously came to pass. Exactly as planned, I did a 10km run in Somalia, a half marathon in Iraq and a full marathon in Afghanistan. In my maritime security work I was well used to assessing risk and taking measures to mitigate it, so not only did I do that with regard to my personal security on these runs, I also did it with my epilepsy, making everyone around me aware of the issue, always knowing where the nearest medical help would be and paying scrupulous attention to my body and what it was telling me. And in the end I was medically fine. I've written in detail about Running Dangerously in *Running For My Life*, so I won't repeat all that here. Suffice it to say there were a good few challenges along the way but also some wonderful times. I got loads of media exposure, including a TV documentary aired on Sky, Virgin and other channels.

In total, the project raised over £100,000 for various charities, the largest beneficiary being War Child, a wonderful organisation that has done amazing work in protecting kids in danger in conflict zones, fighting for their rights and trying to get some sort of basic education for at least some of them. But that task is so enormous and covers such a vast territory that no one charity can possibly deliver on its own. And there is another issue about these very large charities, which as a fundraiser and a donor I began to find difficult to accept: it's nearly impossible to keep track of exactly what is being done with the funds you've provided. I understood that legal red tape, strict procedures and administrative costs had to be involved, not to mention the need to protect the identities of children in hostile environments, but I still found this aspect hard to take. And that's why I soon decided to set up my own small charity, called Frontline Children. We're just a tiny group of trustees, all unpaid volunteers. The downside of being small is that it might limit our growth and even our impact as a charity. But the plus side is that our overheads are almost non-existent, and so every single penny we raise will go directly to the people who need it most. I believe this is much more transparent and ethical, and I'm really proud of that.

I had completed lots of well-documented extreme adventures over the years, but the Running Dangerously expedition was the first major stepping stone in my gradual transition from one kind of life to another. Instead of being a soldier mechanically taking orders from my superiors or a security consultant always answerable to my employers, I was now my own man, making my own choices and completely in charge of my own destiny. And I found it exhilarating. But probably the key importance of these runs in Somalia, Iraq and Afghanistan was to confirm me in my fast-growing belief that this was the path I wanted to take, that new direction I hoped would lead me back to all those values of which I'd once been so proud and which for the past few years had gone out of focus. When I climbed up onto that rooftop in Dubai, I'd pretty much lost sight of the stuff that had always mattered to me. Essentially, I'd almost forgotten who Jordan Wylie was. Running Dangerously was the real start of finding myself again. Rebooting the computer. Resetting the dial.

It was also to be a successful trial run for the even more challenging adventures that lay waiting for me. And one of those had already taken root in my mind. Once again, it was something nobody had done before. Once again, I was told it was a really bad idea. Once again, very politely, I said, 'Rubbish.'

CHAPTER 5

THE GATE OF TEARS

'This chap must be nuts. What the hell does he think he's up to?' I could just imagine some civil servant at their PC in the marbled halls of the Foreign Office in Whitehall, reading my email with their mouth open.

And so I got a polite reply to my enquiry 'strongly advising' me against my project of rowing solo across the Bab el-Mandeb Strait between Djibouti and Yemen. It would be just the same with the other bigwigs from whom I also sought permission: the civil authorities in Djibouti, the local naval commander, the coastguard chief. With varying degrees of vehemence, they all said the same: don't do it. The risks are too great. And we'll have to rescue you if it all goes tits up. Luckily, once they knew I was doing it to shine a light on a good cause and sensed that I wasn't just some wild boy thrill-seeker on an ego trip, their objections muted a little. None of them were exactly happy, though in the end they didn't formally forbid me from doing it. The Djiboutian authorities did a U-turn when they discovered their nation was to be the full beneficiary of the project. They couldn't have been more helpful; it's a funny old world!

But the risks were indeed great, and nobody was more aware of that than me. The Bab el-Mandeb Strait is considered one of the most dangerous sea passages in the world. Its Arabic name translates as 'The Gate of Tears' in memory of all those believed to have drowned in the cataclysmic earthquake that ripped Africa and Asia apart a few thousand years ago. Only 22 miles wide, the strait is the one of the narrowest crossings between the two continents, but a huge volume of the world's shipping squeezes itself through the tight channel, travelling to and from the Suez Canal. Every day, something like 3 million barrels of oil are carried through the crucial gateway. A lone guy in a tiny rowing boat might easily be flattened like a gnat by one of the massive oil tankers or container ships, which wouldn't even realise they had hit him. And though the grimmest days of Somali maritime piracy seemed to be over, there were still a good few 'bad boys' hanging around in these waters, looking for rich pickings – or even just a decent wristwatch and a laptop. Worst of all, though, was the possibility of being kidnapped by terrorists and held hostage for a ransom. Stories like that often had very unhappy endings. No doubt that was what the civil servants in the

Foreign Office were most worried about. No doubt they felt they had enough on their plates without having to deal with something called 'The Jordan Wylie Incident'.

I'd first had the idea of rowing across Bab el-Mandeb in late 2018 after I'd returned from my endurance running project in the Middle East. But as soon as I got back to the UK, a pattern – which sadly was going to become very familiar – reasserted itself and my mental health took a bit of a tumble. Once Running Dangerously had been successfully achieved, once the excitement and thrill had passed, there was suddenly a sense of anti-climax: I was back on my own in the house in Andover, and my world shrank again to those four walls and the rain-soaked pavements of a small English town.

Luckily, the urge inside me not to allow these setbacks to restrict my life remained a very powerful impulse. And there was another element now. Due to the coverage and success of the running project, I'd won quite a large following on social media and was gradually developing a profile as what is now called an 'extreme adventurer'. A few TV appearances on Channel 4's hit shows *Hunted* and *Celebrity Hunted* would speed up that process a lot. I wasn't quite in the Bear Grylls league – far from it in fact – but I was certainly heading in the right direction as far as building my profile as an extreme adventurer trying to help others was concerned. Incredibly, there were now hundreds of thousands of people who knew who I was, and they were keen for more projects too. There's an old showbiz saying that you've got to give your public what they want, and in my case they wanted to read about my next extreme adventure. They sure as hell didn't want to hear that I was moping around my little house, popping pills and looking like an unmade bed.

In short, it was crystal clear by now that it was seriously beneficial for me to have another project lined up as soon as possible after the last one finished. Adventure was my antidote. So, I quickly threw myself into the next crazy gig, the Bab el-Mandeb Strait project now called 'Rowing Dangerously'. I landed a major personal sponsorship partnership with the Eton Harris Group. James, the CEO and founder, has been one of my biggest supporters and has become a best friend too, someone who has been instrumental in keeping my own mental health on track. I owe him a lifetime of thank-yous and much more. Another James (Wilkes), from the maritime security company Gray Page, also became an important stakeholder in the project when his company provided the expedition's main sponsorship funding, 24/7 tracking and remote support for when I was out on the water. His team's knowledge and expertise were invaluable, and his financial support covered all my kit and the team logistics and training too. I drummed up a good deal of media coverage, including a centrefold piece in the *Daily Mail*. And in

February, I started a fun online initiative called 'FebROWary' (get it?), in which people had to row 22 miles on a rowing machine at home or in their gym, the same distance that I'd be rowing across the Bab el-Mandeb Strait. Over 100 people signed up, and I raised around £12,000. A small start but a good one.

Getting the boat was the next major issue. Obviously, an ordinary rowing boat like you use on the Serpentine just wouldn't do. A company called Rannoch made boats for the more serious rower and they now generously supplied two boats – one for my training in the UK; the other for the actual row – and these were eventually gifted and auctioned off for charity after the project. Thanks to Charlie Pitcher, Rannoch's MD, for the very kind support. These were ocean-going coastal rowing boats specifically designed for the modern adventurer, lightweight and fast – exactly what I would need. The boat just needed a name now: *A Million Dreams*. My daughter Evie came up with it: the title of a song from the movie *The Greatest Showman*. I liked that.

Then I had the great good luck of being able to train with Alex Gregory, a double Olympic rowing champion – we are both very proud brand ambassadors for the British luxury watch brand Bremont. We trained at Henley-on-Thames, the iconic site of the world-famous regatta. What I'd omitted to share with Alex till now, and indeed with you, the reader of this book, is that I had never rowed in my life. Never. Not once. Not even on a boating lake in my local park. On our first day, it took Alex about five seconds to realise this when I climbed into the boat facing the wrong way.

'Are you serious, Jordan?'

'Sorry?'

'Christ, this is going to be a long few months,' replied Alex, putting his head in his hands. His pupil didn't even know that you always row with your back facing the direction of travel!

But I began to learn quite quickly, the first lesson being that in rowing a lot of your power comes from your legs, not your arms as you would think. The second thing I learnt was that it takes one hell of a toll on your lower back. I worked with Alex for nearly nine months, eventually going out onto Southampton Water and along the Jurassic Coast of Dorset with its busy shipping lanes and changing tides, where I could encounter some of the conditions I would meet in the Bab el-Mandeb. Fortunately, there are very few pirates operating out of Bournemouth.

But even as I improved under his tutelage, I knew that I was embarking on a row that had never been done before, that not even an Olympic champ like Alex would have considered sensible. Though he never said it out loud, I suspected Alex was thinking the same thing as that guy in the

Foreign Office. 'This guy must be nuts. What the bloody hell does he think he's up to?'

• • •

And so, in October 2019, after nearly a year of planning and training, I flew back to Djibouti to face the perils of the famous Gate of Tears. The most extreme and challenging of all my adventures so far.

I was very glad not to be facing it alone. Along with me came a great guy called Stephen McGrath, a photographer and documentary film-maker. Stephen's trip had been funded by one of my brilliant sponsors, and it was his role to create videos to post on social media, to engage and enthuse as many people as possible and, hopefully, to make them reach into their pockets for charity.

Once in Djibouti City, I scurried around getting the final permissions from the authorities. Yet more long faces. Yet more people who thought it was a really stupid thing to do, worthy cause or not. By now, though, I'd decided there are worse crimes in this life than being crazy. Like sitting on your backside and doing sod all. But I was far from blind to safety and security. I never revealed to anyone the actual date of the row. Sky TV and the BBC wanted me to do a live feed from the boat, but that was just too dangerous. Immediately before the row, I went suddenly silent on social media. Better safe than sorry.

Then the big day came. We hired a 4x4 vehicle with a driver and set off for the starting point of the row: the narrowest part of the strait about eight hours north of the city. My precious boat was tied to the roof rack, but the rough terrain soon made it clear that the boat was getting damaged. We just couldn't take the risk or I might end up sinking to the bottom of the sea and becoming lunch for the local sharks. So back we went to the city and found a fisherman called Mohammed Ali who was prepared to tow the boat to the starting point behind his own vessel. But he wouldn't take us and our kit as well, so with some misgivings we trusted him to keep his word and set out again by road.

If I'd ever needed a reminder about why I was doing this thing, it soon came. On the road, we encountered a long trail of sad, weary refugees. With our driver as interpreter, we discovered that these people were fleeing the conflict in Somalia. But where were they heading? The answer was unbelievable. They were heading for Yemen. Without access to the news media, these poor people were unaware of the war that was ravaging that country and that they were merely marching from one war zone to another. Out of the frying pan into the fire, you might say. Most of them, many barefoot, had been walking for five or six weeks. They slept under trees, had little food and drank water from dirty-looking bottles. Their ultimate goal was eventually to reach the Mediterranean coast and make it over to Europe – if they didn't drown in the attempt. They'd already paid lots of money to the fixers and the people smugglers. Nothing we might have said would have deterred them. It was sobering, heartbreaking stuff. But it was also a spur. OK, I could do nothing to help these tragic people, but I was sure as hell going to help those 250 kids at As Eyla.

To our considerable relief, the fisherman Mohammed Ali had been trustworthy after all, and the boat was now safely beached at the starting point. This was an isolated but spectacular place a few hundred kilometres south of the Eritrean border in the shadow of an amazing mountain called Ras Sayan, which rose sheer from the otherwise flat desert terrain. Shaped like the fin of some giant shark, Ras Sayan was to act as a sort of gigantic lighthouse for me, a marker and reference point I could see from my departure position, and more importantly, it was the location I was to finish at if all went well.

The day of the row dawned clear and warm. I set off at about 5 a.m. The tide was in the right direction, pushing me towards the distant coast of Yemen, just the faintest smudge on the horizon with the sun rising behind it. Stephen had fitted me up with various tracker devices and tiny portable

GoPro cameras to capture the crossing. I had the supplies of food and water we had estimated I would need for the trip. I'd also stocked up on something that might be almost as important: a bit of inspiration. In 1910, American President Theodore 'Teddy' Roosevelt made a famous speech called 'The Man in the Arena', which has been treasured by subsequent generations and especially by soldiers in war zones. Basically, it says to hell with all those who can only criticise from the sidelines and who never actually get up off their arses and try to achieve something that's worth doing. I'd printed out a few lines of this speech and pasted them onto the floor of the boat; I had often carried these words with me on previous expeditions too. 'It is not the critic who counts,' Roosevelt had said. 'The credit belongs to the man who is actually in the arena, whose face is marred by dust and sweat and blood.' Well said, Teddy. You nailed it, mate.

After all the long months of planning and training, this was it. I got into the boat and rowed away from the beach, waved off by Stephen plus a few bemused locals and their scruffy dogs. For a moment, I felt very lonely indeed. From my years in maritime security, I already knew that the sea could be the loneliest place on earth. Back then, however, I'd been on a 10,000-ton container ship with my friends around me, a comfy cabin, a decent loo and a chef employed to cook my meals. Now, there was just a lightweight rowing boat, a few bottles of water, some basic nourishment and my bloody-minded determination to do this thing and also raise two fingers to everybody who had told me it was an impossible and very dangerous mission. But the weather was perfect and the water reasonably calm so that the dreaded Gate of Tears looked extremely beautiful. What's more, I felt totally fit, not just physically but mentally too. I might not have been the world's best rower, but I'd been training hard all these months with one of them. Still, I was certainly aware of being a very long way from Henley-on-Thames.

Sure enough, it wasn't long before I began to see the massive oil tankers and container ships looming up towards me like great monsters risen from the deep. I'd spent so many years working on these vessels that I could easily picture the guys on board them right now, waking up in those comfy cabins, going to the galley for their bacon and eggs, starting their day on the upper decks. They'd be scanning the sea for the smallest sign of anything suspicious on the water and continually checking their radars. My problem was that I was just too damn small to register on those radars as anything more than the frothy crest of a wave, and if I got too close I might be joining all those poor drowned folk who'd gone under when the earthquake had severed the two ancient continents. So I really hoped those guys on the bridge with the binoculars were wide awake.

Yet I knew that my major risk wasn't from the gargantuan ships but from the 'bad boys' of these waters. From simply being in the wrong place at the wrong time. Just asking to be kidnapped. It was a comfort that I was being remotely monitored by Inmarsat, the satellite communications company, and expedition sponsors Gray Page, but if push came to shove, all they'd be able to do would be to alert the Djibouti rescue services and the military in the region. Then I would indeed become 'The Jordan Wylie Incident', with those Foreign Office guys in London shaking their heads and calling me all sorts of names.

As the sun rose against my back, I was making pretty good progress. The Bab el-Mandeb Strait is notorious for its tricky tides and treacherous undercurrents, but it seemed to be behaving itself so far. Maybe it knew I was doing this for a good reason. But then the first pain started. Oh God. And then another. Deep down in my lower belly. It could only mean one thing. I groaned when I remembered what I'd thoughtlessly eaten the night before; it was now pretty obvious that something hadn't been properly cooked on the campfire. It was just as well nobody could hear the string of expletives I let fly across the water. In order not to offend any squeamish readers I'll gloss over what happened next, but it wasn't pretty. Let me just say that sticking one's derrière over the edge of the boat wasn't an option in case I had it bitten off by a shark or capsized. Use your imagination for the rest. Or perhaps not.

All through the voyage, I was very much on my guard, especially when, after about five hours, I got near to the small island of Perim, a few miles off the coast of mainland Yemen. Since this island is Yemeni land, I'd already decided this was as far as I'd go. I had contacted the Yemeni authorities explaining that this was a row for a charitable cause, but that hadn't cut any ice and I'd been flatly refused permission to land on their territory. I was also aware that there are lots of legalities around landing in Yemen, so I knew from the outset there would be no nice long lunch on a sunny Yemeni beach, resting my aching back and arms and sending my daughter a postcard from Yemen. For the entire trip, I'd not be able to get out of the boat. Not that I'd have been too tempted anyway. For 100 years or more, the island of Perim had been under British control as a dependency of Aden and was used as an important coaling station by the vast number of ships going to and from Suez. Now Perim is part of Yemen, though, Brits aren't quite as welcome as we once were. As I approached the island, I could clearly see what appeared to be some sort of military camp, and it was perfectly possible that I'd already been spotted. So, I decided to turn tail and scuttle out of there as fast as my oars would allow me.

But I'd made it to Yemen. I'd crossed the Gate of Tears. Now let's see if I could make it back.

However, the return trip was destined to be much longer and much harder. The wind had changed direction and the tide was pushing me southwards, meaning I had to row against it in a north-westerly direction to make it back to the lighthouse of the Ras Sayan mountain in Djibouti. By now it was late morning and the sun was at its zenith. I was getting hotter and thirstier and had a lot less energy than I'd started out with.

I have sometimes been asked what I thought about during those long hours across the Bab el-Mandeb Strait. Was I thinking of home? Of my daughter Evie in Andover and my mum and dad in Blackpool? I confess it was none of that. My mind had flicked a switch and the soldier in me had kicked in again. Nice, warm, human emotions have no place in any situation that might be dangerous; they cloud judgement, weaken focus and affect decision-making. There's a technique called 'Actions On', which military men and women apply in any potentially dodgy scenario. It's all about assessing the risk. Evaluating the potential enemy around you. Deciding how you'll react in the face of any of a spectrum of possible outcomes. Always asking yourself 'What if? What if?' It's so ingrained in me now that I even do it on passenger planes when going on my hols overseas. I never sleep on a plane. Instead, I quietly glance around me, wondering who might be the most likely cause of trouble and who else might assist me in the event of an incident. It might sound a bit over the top, but I can't help it. As the saying goes, you can take the boy out of the army but you can't take the army out of the boy.

Luckily, my 'Actions On' instinct was on red alert as I pulled myself back towards Djibouti. Because what I'd feared most suddenly came to pass. Out of nowhere, a small skiff zoomed towards me with several men on board. It looked like the 'bad boys' had arrived. I had a sudden mental flash of being held hostage in a rat-infested hellhole for the next few months, or even years. The shits I'd had earlier in the day were as nothing compared to the ones I started having now. The big question was how 'bad' these boys were. Who exactly were they? Just harmless fishermen? Yemeni coastguards? Djibouti military? Pirates? Terrorists? And what did they want? Was it just the wristwatch and the laptop, or was it a stonking ransom that the British government would refuse to pay? As the skiff got nearer, my heart rate went through the roof. Especially when I saw their weapons.

One of the men spoke a few words of English. They claimed to be security guards, but my gut told me that wasn't the truth. What was I doing there? Where was I going? As my rowing boat rocked on the waves their skiff had stirred up, I waited with my heart in my mouth while these guys eyed up what I might have of value. In the end, I was ordered to hand over two of the tiny GoPro cameras they had spotted and a bottle of water, then they zoomed off as quickly as they'd come. And that was it. End of drama. To this day, I'm still not sure who these armed men really were. Probably they were just petty thieves and chancers. So I'd been extremely lucky. 'The Jordan Wylie Incident' didn't happen. But it might easily have, and my life might have been changed for ever in those few minutes.

Although a bit shaken up, I just kept on pulling on the oars back towards Djibouti. The tide was still against me, and the sea was much choppier than it had been that morning. I was sick over the side a few times, but better that part of my body than the other end. By now, though, my water supply was almost gone, which is never good news when you've been losing fluid from both ends. The sun was beginning to set before I finally saw the shark-fin Ras Sayan mountain rising on the horizon. Boy, was I happy to see it. I'd been rowing for over twelve hours; five out and seven back.

Stephen was supposed to be waiting for me in the support boat in order to film the successful conclusion of the row. But somehow our communications had been crossed and he wasn't there due to some technical issues with his engine, so

I had to wait at Ras Sayan for a few hours. There, I had my second encounter of the day with a bunch of heavies; this time the Djibouti coastguard. I used my basic French, some phone calls were made and it was smoothed over.

That night I slept like the dead, and I woke up the next day with my body aching in every muscle, tendon and ligament. But I'd done it. They'd all said I couldn't, or shouldn't, but I had. The guy who'd never even rowed off Blackpool Beach had rowed across one of the most dangerous waterways in the world and lived to tell the tale.

But I had decided long before that I wasn't going to tell that tale till I was well out of Djibouti. Security considerations had to remain, even after the event. Ructions might still happen. So, it wasn't till I reached the sanctuary of a comfy hotel in Dubai that I spread the word on social media that Rowing Dangerously, my most extreme adventure yet, had been achieved. Now I could call my parents and my daughter to let them know that the good ship *A Million Dreams* had made it and that I was safe. The media now descended, and I undertook as much publicity as I could possibly get, as this always increased charity donations. Unfortunately, the folks at Guinness World Records twice rejected my application for inclusion. Since nobody else had done it before me, I hadn't actually broken a record, merely established my own timing.

Guinness thought it very unlikely anyone else would ever make another attempt due to the risks involved, and so that was that.

It would have been nice for my sponsors, but I wasn't really that bothered, to be honest. As always, I tried to remember my reason why. It wasn't about Jordan Wylie's ego trip; it was to build that school. Nothing else really mattered. And on the drive back to Djibouti City, that imperative had again hit home to me. For the second time, we came across that harrowing column of exhausted refugees, still trudging in their tragic ignorance towards Yemen and whatever fate might await them there.

In the end, my row across the Gate of Tears would raise about $150,000 towards the school. Not a bad start. But there was still a very long way to go before Ibrahim, his sisters and the rest of those 250 kids could walk into school on their first day. So, even before I got back to the UK, my mind was churning away. OK, what now? What's my next adventure? To raise more cash, I knew it needed to grab even more attention than Rowing Dangerously. As yet, I had no idea what that might be. When it eventually came to me, I found it ironic that for over twelve hours on the Bab el-Mandeb Strait, I had literally held the answer in my hand. It was a long, thin piece of carbon. An oar. Or, as it is known in other contexts, a paddle.

CHAPTER 6

BRASS MONKEYS

It was one of the weirdest evenings of my life, and I've had my share of those. I was sitting watching a young boy receive a prize. Not for reciting poetry or for winning the high jump but for something which in most other places would have seemed totally bizarre, not to mention illegal. This kid had a shotgun over his shoulder and was getting an award for shooting dead a moose as his family and friends cheered him on. He can't have been much more than ten or so, but he was already an expert hunter, able to discuss the merits of different firearms and how to slaughter various species of wild animal. In the UK, an evening like this one was simply inconceivable. The authorities would have freaked out. There would have been protesters shouting abuse outside. In my home town of Blackpool, the police would have been involved, the parents prosecuted and the kid dragged into care by social services.

But this was a long way from the UK, further even from my usual stomping ground of Africa and the Middle East. This was Yukon in north-west Canada and about as different from any of those places as it is possible to be. Sitting next door to Alaska, Yukon is a wilderness. An incredibly beautiful landscape of snow-crowned mountains, dense forests and torrential rivers, it has one of the sparsest populations anywhere, with only 35,000 people in the whole province. And no wonder. Living in Yukon breeds a certain type of man, woman and child. Folk here need to be tough, resilient and indomitable. In their own way, they are as unlike us privileged Europeans as are the troubled peoples of much of Africa and the Middle East.

Yet that very difference is why I was there. My military career and security work had opened up the wider world to me in ways that few other jobs ever could have. I'd grown addicted to exploring countries, peoples and cultures that were alien to my own. The travel bug had bitten me good and proper and there seemed to be no antidote. So, after I'd returned to the UK from rowing across the Bab el-Mandeb, I decided to raise the next tranche of money for the school at As Eyla by running another series of marathons. This time it would be nothing like the sweltering, semi-tropical countries I was used to running in. This time, my unique selling proposition would be to run in polar climates. Now, my adversary wouldn't be extreme heat but extreme cold. I'd christened the project 'Running Dangerously – The Polar Edition'.

So, in January 2020, me and my adventurer friend Sally Orange found ourselves as honoured guests at Yukon's Annual Fish and Game Dinner and Awards Night, the hottest ticket in town. About 500 people, all dolled up, crammed into a big hall in Whitehorse, the Yukon capital. The walls were decorated with the heads of long-dead moose, deer, elk, caribou and bears, while a large number of their relations, only recently passed away, were carried over shoulders towards the kitchens. I thought of my sister, a devoted vegan, who would probably have thrown up the moment she walked into the room. As alien cultures go, this was certainly it.

So, there was this kid with his shotgun, up on stage describing in grisly detail exactly how he had tracked and dispatched the deer or the moose to pastures new. Loud applause from the audience. Mum and Dad with tears in their eyes. It was like the Meat Eaters Oscar night.

That evening, it wasn't for Sally and me to judge this boy nor his parents nor the culture in which he was growing up. Yukon is a wilderness environment, and the psyche of the hunter-gatherer has always been necessary for their very survival. And though the modern world with its awesome advances in technology means life there is in some ways easier than it was for their forefathers, that carnivorous attitude is still bred in the bone and passed on down the generations. It brought home to me yet again how much the accident of where we are born shapes our lives. The ten-year-old child in Yukon embracing and loving his guns; the children of the damaged countries of Africa and the Middle East fleeing in terror from the worst that guns can do. Yet both living in places where a certain toughness is absorbed with mother's milk, where very little comes easy. War and peace. Tropical heat and arctic cold. It doesn't really matter. It's all about how you meet the challenges that come your way and somehow make the best of it.

•   •   •

Running Dangerously – The Polar Edition was planned to be a series of ten marathons in some of the coldest places on the planet – of course places I wanted to visit too. In order, I'd take part in events in Siberia, Yukon, Alaska, Iceland, Mongolia, Lapland, Svalbard and the Falklands, culminating in trips to both the iconic North Pole and Antarctica. Once again, I generated as much media interest as possible and then searched for sponsors. The usual practice is to get your sponsors first and then alert the media, but I have always found it works far better the other way around. Partly due to my appearances on *Hunted*, my social media profile was still increasing all the time, and once again the response was encouraging. In particular, my great friend James from the Eton Harris Group continued his incredible support. Although he is based outside the UK, we would speak each week by phone, and I would go out to see him in the Middle East anytime I could. He really wanted to support the efforts of Frontline Children and see those kids go to school just as much as I did. Many corporate charitable sponsors are primarily concerned with their brand awareness, hoping for a bit of reflected glory from their involvement with a worthy cause. Fair enough. But I have never got that sense from James and the support of him, his family and his staff has always been a big element in spurring me on.

As with all my adventure projects, I knew that I would only get out what I put in. So I had to train hard. I'd not experienced extreme cold before; the biting winter wind on Blackpool Prom probably didn't count, and my love of cold showers and winter wild river swims wouldn't quite cut the mustard either. But something attracted me to it and not just as a dramatic contrast to the hot, dusty countries where I'd always run before. As a lad, I'd always been stirred by the stories of Arctic explorers like Sir Ranulph Fiennes and, going way back, of Sir Ernest Shackleton, Roald Amundsen, Ann Bancroft and Captain Scott. I'd never forgotten the tragic end to Scott's Antarctic expedition of 1912, when the doomed

Captain Oates had left the tent to die in the blizzard. 'I'm just going outside and may be some time.' Not wanting to share that fate, I knew I'd better do my homework and prepare myself for the toughest physical conditions I'd ever faced.

I arranged to train in a cryo-chamber at the Extreme Environments Laboratory at the University of Portsmouth. This was run by Professor Mike Tipton, a world-renowned expert on the effects of adverse environments on both body and mind and how to prepare and protect those who go into such places. A cryo-chamber is about the size of a shipping container, inside which the temperature can be lowered to simulate those of extremely cold climates. The first time I went inside it, and despite being dressed in the appropriate insulated kit, I let go a string of silent expletives as I felt my privates shrink to the size of two garden peas and a prawn. My teeth started chattering furiously, asking one another what the hell I thought I was doing. Imagine jumping into an ice-cold pool, then multiply it about a hundred times and you'll get some idea. On top of that, there were big fans creating the wind chill factor. You can't stay inside a cryo-chamber for long – at first not more than just a few minutes – but your body gradually makes the adjustments it needs to make, and the process becomes more bearable. Everyone's body reacts slightly differently, so it's important to get to know what your own particular system can cope with. While inside, you're doing the usual training exercises – running on a treadmill or on the spot, doing press-ups and squats. One of the first lessons you learn is the importance of keeping your water bottle inside your kit close to your body; otherwise it freezes over and you'll dehydrate. The goal is gradually to build up to an hour or more inside the ice box, and when you come out again the temperature of an ordinary room feels like a heatwave.

Apart from climatising my body to extreme cold, the other big consideration was the difference between running on hard ground and running on snow, the latter giving way slightly under the feet and so putting tension on the legs in unusual ways. A different ballgame altogether. So, I started training on beaches, the softness of the sand making it a perfect stand-in for the white stuff.

With generous sponsorship in place, the media really interested and the basic training completed, I was eager to get started as soon as possible. This was mostly because of the overarching need to keep sending money out to Djibouti, but as always there was something else too. When I returned to my home in Andover after completing my rowing challenge, the black dog came barking at my door again and my mental health took a dive. Easy to see why, of course. Despite all its dangers, the beauty and warmth of the strait seemed a whole lot more appealing than a small English town in the grey, wet midwinter. The more I planned and trained and lost myself in the preparations for my next adventure, the more I could keep the black dog at bay.

But my mental health wasn't the only issue. The mild epilepsy I'd suffered not long ago meant that my GP refused to complete the medical forms that the organisers of most of the marathons I'd lined up required for entry. So once again, I tracked down a private GP who was willing. Many doctors, for obvious, well-meaning reasons, tend to be highly risk averse. Luckily, some are more empathetic, especially if they've got some experience of athletes, adventurers and people with military training. I found a lovely doctor in my local town called Dr Rome Begum. She was always very helpful and understanding and took the time to understand the issues and challenges before just writing me off like my old GP seemed to do. Dr Begum became a great source of knowledge and help, and she offered remote medical advice for me and my teams on other expeditions too, which was greatly appreciated.

I then made a silly mistake. I decided to try snowboarding for the first time and flew out to the Sierra Nevada in southern Spain with some friends. On Day 1, I fell flat on my arse and fractured my coccyx. That's the little bone at the lower tip of your spine and is a bony remnant of when human beings had tails. Many people don't know of it, but if you fracture it, you sure as hell get to know it fast 'cause it hurts like hell. For the next six weeks I rested it as well as I could, but when the time came to fly out for the first marathon on my list, my tailbone was still throbbing.

The first marathon was to be run in Siberia. A place whose name alone slightly chills the heart. But, in fact, it was to be the easy one, just a warm-up half marathon and a perfect start to Running Dangerously – The Polar Edition. But getting there wasn't easy at all. At the Russian Embassy in London, where I had to go to get the necessary visa, the hatchet-faced woman refused to believe my reason for going to Siberia and was quite certain I was off to find myself a young Russian bride and carry her back to Andover as some sort of a domestic and sexual slave. All the Russians I encountered seemed completely obsessed with rules and regulations, as if they were binding red tape around my legs before I'd even started to run.

But eventually, after three connecting flights, I finally made it to the city of Omsk, where the famous Siberian Ice Half Marathon takes place every year on Russian Christmas Day. Though it was -19 degrees and the city was snowbound, the streets on the race route had been cleared, and since we ran past supermarkets and branches of McDonald's, there was little chance of suffering the same fate as poor Captain Oates. In fact, the race wasn't nearly as challenging as I'd expected; I coped not too badly with the cold and finished the distance in a reasonable time, even though the time was never a concern. The only concern was raising money. The worst part of it was my coccyx, which seemed uninterested in my charitable endeavours and continued to pulsate for the whole damn way.

The Siberian race attracted several thousand runners from all over the world, some of whom came almost every year. I soon met a bloke from Stoke-on-Trent and another from Liverpool. But the most important person I got to know on my trip was a remarkable woman called Sally Orange, who was to become a good friend and running buddy.

Sally and I had connected just before I headed for Siberia. She had read about my project and asked if she could come along and run with me. Sally was a very experienced marathon runner. Ex-military, she had been an officer in the Army Medical Corps and, now retired from the services, she worked as a physiotherapist helping to rehabilitate injured veterans from Afghanistan. But the special thing about Sally was what she was doing with her time now she was no longer in the military. Suffering from severe depression and chronic anxiety, she had been discharged from the life she loved and now dedicated herself to encouraging discussion about these issues and helping those who had fallen prey to them.

If that all sounds a bit heavy, it didn't come across that way. Because Sally Orange lived up to her name. She was the only person to have run a marathon on every continent in fancy dress – always as a piece of fruit. Her strategy was to promote healthy eating, a valuable aspect of good mental health. Sadly, the organisers of some runs didn't like this at all. They felt that fancy dress somehow diminished their marathons as serious athletic or extreme adventure events. Being amateur was fine; for many people, looking amateur wasn't. This hurt Sally a bit, but she shrugged it off because her 'silly' costumes often pulled her into the spotlight, which might not otherwise have happened among the huge numbers running each race. It made people ask her the reason why she was dressed as a banana, which then gave her the opportunity to talk about mental health and why it really matters to bring it into that spotlight. She is fearless, committed and also making a difference.

In Siberia, Sally asked me to run in fancy dress too. Despite the good cause and how close it was to me personally, I guess stupid vanity made me resist at first. I didn't really want to look like a complete idiot all over social media, dressed up as a cucumber. In the end we agreed that I would run as a character called 'Kristoff' from Disney's film *Frozen*. In the movie, Kristoff is a character who talks openly about his innermost thoughts and feelings – exactly what Sally's mission was to encourage people to do – and not at all like the usual strong, silent Prince Charming. So, Sally dressed as Queen Elsa and together we took to the streets of Omsk. We made a great team.

Back home, there was plenty more media coverage, both mainstream and online. I did some talks in schools too, and there was no doubt that my Kristoff costume had won attention, so I had to admit Sally had a point after all. In the end, the Siberian Ice Half Marathon brought about £10k into the coffers, but it didn't stay there long. Off it went to Djibouti as quickly as it came in. All the time this was the urgent imperative in my mind. If the money stopped coming from me, the building of the school would stop too. That meant that the workers, most of whom lived and slept on site, would swiftly evaporate looking for other work wherever it might be, and the construction would be abandoned. The wind would whistle through the half-built windows and doors, and the Minister of Education's cynicism would be justified. In that posh office of his, he would shrug and say, 'I told you so.' And I bloody well wasn't having that.

• • •

'Hey, buddy, are you from Lancashire, England?' the taxi driver asked.

'Wow. Yeah. How on earth did you guess that?' I replied.

'I recognise the accent,' he said.

'You've been to Lancashire?'

'Nope. But a guy from somewhere called Preston is a bit of a celebrity over here,' he replied. 'He wrote our most famous poem, called "The Law of the Yukon". I learnt it at school and I can still quote bits of it.'

And he then proceeded to do so as the taxi drove from the airport into town. It was stirring stuff, but not exactly encouraging. Scary, in fact. Written by Robert Service, a poet at one time as well-known as Rudyard Kipling, it came from the period of the famous Klondike Gold Rush of 1897 and celebrated those brave souls who travelled from all round the world in the hope of making their fortunes. 'Send only your strong and sane,' Service says, warning that all others will perish. Crikey. And presumably just as relevant to marathon runners in 2020. Maybe I should get the poem embossed on a T-shirt sometime. I'd already sensed that the poet didn't exaggerate. According to the temperature gauge on the dashboard, it was -28 degrees outside. In the few moments between leaving the airport terminal and getting into the cab, I'd felt the hairs in my nostrils freeze and realised that this was going to be a far tougher gig than Siberia.

It was dark outside by now, and most of the citizens of Whitehorse were snuggled up inside their homes. Yet the streets were not entirely deserted: here and there, I would suddenly glimpse large, shadowy shapes moving between the buildings or loitering in alleyways. 'That's just the moose,' said the driver. 'In Yukon, there are three of them for every human being. They mostly come out at night. They won't bother you unless you bother them. But they can be aggressive not-so-little creatures, so I don't advise trying to cuddle one.'

That was just the tip of the iceberg. Along the streets, in among the usual traffic signs were others warning you to 'beware of grizzly bears'. I noticed that the message specified it was 'grizzly' bears you had to be aware of. Knowing very little about bears, I wondered if 'grizzly' just meant 'grumpy' and that you'd be fine if you met up with a bear who seemed to be in a good mood. A bear who was, forgive the gag, totally chilled. I decided I would never try to find out. But I was certainly a long way from Blackpool Prom, where the grizzliest creature you'd meet would be an angry drunk on a Saturday night.

Whitehorse is the capital of the province of Yukon. It has the nickname Wilderness City, but with a population of only about 25,000, the word 'city' is pushing it a bit. Still, it is the only settlement of much size in the territory and also its warmest place; the average winter temperature in daytime is a sweltering -19 degrees, which I guess makes it the Cairo of Yukon. But it is an attractive enough town, splayed out along the banks of the great Yukon river and encircled by a necklace of snow-capped mountains.

To my delight, the indefatigable fruit lady Sally Orange had said she'd love to join me for a second time, and I was glad of her company. But the Yukon race was a much more serious undertaking than the Siberian one. It was also far more dangerous. In previous years, people had lost limbs due to frostbite from the intense cold. Even seasoned runners, experienced in marathons around the globe, were just not prepared for the brutality of these temperatures. They read the statistics in advance, but when they got there the reality of it was something else. Strong men and women quaked in their new snow boots.

The Yukon race is an umbrella title for what is in fact four events of differing levels of challenge. The one-day marathon, which I'd signed up for, is by far the easiest option, if there ever was one. Above that come three races of 100, 300 and 430km each. For the highest two categories, the organisers require some assurance that the entrants have done some pretty serious training. At these levels, it isn't so much a marathon as a mini-expedition in which you have to be able to self-sustain on your journey across spectacular but treacherous terrain. In the higher levels, competitors can choose to run, ski or use a 'fat bike', which is an off-road bicycle with oversized tyres

designed for use on snow, sand, mud and other unstable sur-
faces. But the word 'race' is really a misnomer in these conditions. The reality was that absolutely nobody was going to be
covering the ground like greased lightning.

Due to the geographical remoteness of Yukon, plus the
complexity and expense of actually getting there, the number
of entrants was not high compared to the marathons I'd
taken part in up till now. In total, there were no more than
about fifty people entered across the four levels. But what
the Yukon race lacked in numbers, it made up for in the cali-
bre of those taking part. People who flew into Whitehorse
tended to be a bunch of tough cookies. About 30 per cent
were women, one in her sixties. One guy was in his seventies,
an old-age pensioner who was entered for the 100km option.
He had already tried a couple of times and was back again,
determined to do it this time. Clearly, the bowling green
held no charms for him. Awesome. Like him, many of the
competitors had been here before, often at the lowest level,
and were now back to push themselves further up the scale.
Maybe they'd tried and failed before and that had really got
to them, like an itch they just had to scratch. Some had been
training hard for the past year in order to return and face the
special challenges of Yukon and this time beat the bastard. It
was unfinished business.

There were several military or ex-military types, whom I

could nearly always sniff out. Something about an attitude, a focus, a discipline that they exuded almost like sweat. One Danish man had served in Iraq at the same time as me, something which always triggers an instant and powerful bond. There were also the 'extreme adventurers' like me, looking for a 'life less ordinary'. Most of the runners were billeted in the same hotel, and most evenings the bar boasted the most fascinating cross-section of people I'd ever met.

I began to feel a bit inadequate compared to some of these folk, since I was just doing the basic marathon. It even began to seem a bit wimpish, and I briefly thought about moving up a notch to the 100km event. It was just that old macho crap kicking in, but I used my intelligence. I'd never run in anything remotely like these conditions, and it would have been sheer bloody stupidity to over-reach myself. Luckily, I'd long since learnt the wisdom of always keeping my goal in sight, which, in this instance, was to raise money for the school in Djibouti, not to end up frozen to death like Captain Oates. On previous Yukon races, people on the tough levels hadn't just lost frostbitten limbs but had also lost their reason, becoming delirious with cold and even stripping off all their clothes. Not good stuff to hear about. A man called Alex de Saint, a famous marathon runner and waterman, said to me in the bar: 'In Yukon, nobody is bigger than nature.' Another lesson I needed to learn, and fast.

For the marathon, the organisers had tried to lay out a rough track with a Ski-Doo, which is a bit like a jet-ski for use on snow. How much of that track might disappear under fresh snowfall was the unpredictable element, though there would also be some marker posts along the route. In this wild environment, safety always had to be a prime consideration. With no mobile phone signal on the route, we all had to carry a satellite phone plus a location tracker device. There were various rendezvous points along the way, so if somebody didn't show up at that point after a reasonable amount of time, the organisers could instigate a search. Unlike back in Omsk, there certainly wouldn't be any McDonald's.

Sally and I were wearing much heavier clothing and headwear than had been necessary in Siberia. But it was important not to overdo that. The most vital thing was to try to control your body temperature. If you were too cold, you risked frostbite and possible mental confusion. But too hot and the sweat on your body could then freeze. It would be as if you were encased inside an ice cube, and that is very dangerous indeed. So it was a delicate balancing act. Sally of course managed to incorporate a degree of fancy dress; this time she was a grapefruit! As always, her strategy worked. Why are you dressed like that? they all asked. Yet another opportunity to spread her gospel of the importance of looking after the spirit as well as the body.

But however threatening Yukon might be, it was also devastatingly beautiful. The rushing rivers, the dense forests of snowy trees, the mountain ranges jagged against the deep-blue sky. Above all, the air was of a purity I'd never experienced before. Like a glass of cold water pouring down the throat. A tonic to the body. My lungs must have loved it. There was simply no pollution. A magical feeling.

On the day of the event, I soon learnt the major fact about this 'run': actual running is impossible. In the hotel bar, I had been warned about this by the old hands, but I hadn't listened. That old macho crap again. Like a prat, I let myself forget Alex de Saint's dictum that, in this wild land, nature sets the rules. Within half an hour of the start, my quads and calves were aching. My training back home on soft beach sand just hadn't prepared me for the toll this unforgiving terrain was determined to put on my body. So I had to rein in my enthusiasm pretty quick. Don't be a plonker. Be careful. Slow down. Too fast and I might lose control of my body temperature, go a bit bonkers and strip off in the snow. Get arrested for indecent exposure.

Throughout the marathon, the snowfall was constant, though by Yukon standards it was apparently no more than a drizzle. But sure enough the track laid out by the Ski-Doo was soon partly obscured by the fresh fall, so the orange marker posts were a godsend. This experience was so different from that in Siberia. Instead of being surrounded by masses of other runners, I was pretty much alone for most of it. Now and again, I'd spot one of the other ten entrants either ahead of or behind me, but for most of the 26.2 miles it was a solitary experience. On a human level, anyway. Through the curtain of snow, I often saw the deer and moose, though I remembered the taxi driver's warning and didn't stop to stroke them or tickle them under the chin. (And luckily the bears, 'grizzly' or not, seemed to have stayed at home that day.) Of course, they did make a wonderful sight, these majestic creatures of the wilderness, standing out against the blinding white of the landscape, their antlers held high as if in defiance of whatever nature could throw at them. Awesome.

Eventually, Sally and I somehow managed to meet up and keep each other going for the final few miles. The entrants had been allowed twelve hours to complete the course and I did it in half that time, which wasn't too bad at all. Job well done. And, an excellent bonus, my nuts hadn't frozen off.

But it was good to get back to the warmth of the hotel. Sally and I were both pretty knackered, and it would have been great to just hang out in the bar and have a bloody good dinner. But before leaving the UK, I'd contacted the Canadian Army Cadets, which is affiliated to the UK Army Cadet Force, and had agreed, a bit unwisely perhaps, to give a talk that very same night to a bunch of the cadets. But somehow, buoyed up by the kindness of everyone I met there, I got a second wind and had a great night. And it was there that one of the parents invited Sally and me to the Meat Eaters Oscar night. Whatever I thought of their dietary habits, we found the Yukon folk extraordinarily warm and welcoming. Maybe there's some correlation between living in a cold climate and having a warm heart. And ultimately that's what makes those few days in Yukon such a happy memory. The running element of the Yukon trip brought me something almost as valuable: it was another priceless lesson in the definition of success and failure.

After our own marathon, we stayed on for a few more days, waiting for the complicated flights we'd booked to take us home. Back into the hotel in dribs and drabs came some of those who had entered the much tougher levels of the Yukon race. Only about fifteen of them had managed to complete their different challenges, and only two heroes had finished the 430km course. So, some very deflated people trudged back into the hotel bar to drown their sorrows. They'd had a far tougher time than Sally and me. Sleeping out in the wilderness, carrying food supplies, struggling to erect tents and build fires while the snow came down. Most of them were exhausted. Some still shivering. Nearly all of them a bit gutted. Tired and emotional before they'd touched a drop of alcohol. One poor guy, who had been trying to raise money for Great

Ormond Street Children's Hospital, was really distraught. I tried my best to cheer him up and to remind him that failure is a relative thing. He'd trained hard, been dedicated and committed, and in all of that he'd been a success. He wasn't one of the arrogant egotists you often meet on these marathons, though there were very few of that type here. He'd maybe just been a bit unrealistic about his abilities in this terrain. Perhaps if he could learn the lessons about why he'd not achieved his goal, then he could come back next year and have another go.

But within hours, I stopped practising what I preached and did something that was pretty damn risky myself. Daft as it sounds, I'd not really realised just how close Yukon is to Alaska, one of the other destinations I'd listed for Running Dangerously – The Polar Edition. From the city of Whitehorse, travelling over the border from Canada into the USA would be a road trip of no more than a few hours. Why fly back to the UK then come all the way out again in the near future? Think of the money I'd save.

The hotel staff checked out the weather for us. The road across the border had been closed by an avalanche but was now open again. So, Sally and I got up at the crack of dawn, hired a car and set off. It was snowing, of course, but we were used to that by now. The scenery was incredible. One long straight road between mountain ranges – like something the Romans might have built if they'd ever got this far. We only saw three other cars the whole way. The big risk was of a really major snowfall, getting snowed up in Alaska and missing our flights back to the UK from Yukon. That'd be a real screw-up and no mistake.

At the American border, the guard clearly thought we were nuts, but he was another guy who'd served in Iraq with the US Marines, so that eased our passage. We made it to the town of Skagway, which, like Whitehorse, is another of the famous Gold Rush towns. I'd never seen anything like Skagway. It was like a time-capsule of the late nineteenth century, like something out of a movie with its cowboy saloon and wooden posts on which to tether horses. At first, I couldn't make up my mind if it was real or actually some sort of Disney theme park parody. In the long days of summer, this was a bustling destination for tourist cruise ships, but in midwinter it was a ghost town, half-buried under snow, its streets deserted. A solitary woman walking a dog was amazed to see us. On top of our thermals, we'd decided to wear military uniform to promote the Army Cadets around the world and do some live feeds on social media for the young people back home to follow our adventure, so maybe she thought the Brits were invading the USA. But apart from her and a couple who ran a hardware store, we didn't see a single soul. The folk in the shop warned us that a new avalanche was predicted, and the snow was getting heavier all the time. Our simple plan had been to run the 26.2 miles marathon distance around the streets of the town. But after running about 10 miles, the snow was above our boots and we did a reality check. If we wanted to get back to Yukon, we needed to stop right now and head back. There would be no time for postcards from Alaska.

But now things got very scary, though Sally and I maintained our stiff military discipline in front of one another. Now the tarmac and the road markings had vanished completely and we could only judge the sides of the roads by the line of the trees. Back at the border, the guard strongly suggested we go no further and return to Skagway, but we had to get back to Whitehorse or we'd miss our flights. So we left him in the rear-view mirror scratching his head at these crazy English people.

But we were certainly now in real danger. We got some reassurance from the fact that we had tracker devices, so people back in Whitehorse had an idea of our location. But we were now in a 'whiteout', when the snow is so thick that you're more or less blinded, both by the light of it and by the loss of the vital sense of where you are. Disorientated. Your senses not quite working the way they usually do. Above all, the real fear of the car being blown off the road or of another sudden avalanche. Being buried alive in a car, freezing to death and maybe not being found for days wasn't the way either Sally or I wanted to depart this life. But luckily, that good old military discipline held. We didn't panic. And, thank Christ, the conditions slowly improved. The avalanche never happened, and we made it back to Whitehorse just as the dark descended. Later, we heard that an avalanche had indeed closed that road again just after we'd passed through. Half an hour later and we might well have been caught in it. We might not have lived to tell this tale.

But obviously we did. And despite having 'failed' to complete our Alaskan marathon, the real objective had been achieved: getting people's attention and persuading them to donate to the school in Africa. Usually, most of our donations came in during the events rather than afterwards, as people were able to follow us on social media and donate on the spot. In total, the Yukon and Alaskan efforts raised another £8k. Once again, as soon as the money came in, it went out – straight to the project manager in Djibouti. More bricks, more mortar, more joists, more doors and window frames, more tiles for the roof. All the time, the shadow of the school growing larger against the tropical sun. I kept that image in my mind.

As soon as I got back home to Andover, the phone rang. The voice on the other end announced itself as being from NATO. My first thought was that somebody was taking the piss. My second thought was, 'Christ, what have I done?' With my 'bad boy' history, I instantly imagined that Sally and I had broken some law or regulation back in Yukon and caused a diplomatic incident. Maybe running in our uniforms? But the man on the phone really was the head of NATO press and media, and it turned out that NATO was pleased with me. They'd been following me online, had been impressed by my Army Cadet involvement and now wanted to harness my social media presence to help them to push their message to a younger, more diverse audience. NATO was about to launch its biggest ever exercise in the Arctic Circle, teaching its troops how to defend the region in the event of a Russian attack. It would be called Exercise Cold Response. Would I like to go to Norway as an observer/reporter, to run my next marathon there and then spread the word with blogs and interviews on social media? No fee, but everything else paid for and VIP treatment. It was a no-brainer. You bet I'd like to go.

The arrangements were swiftly put in place. Stephen, the film-maker who'd been with me on my row across the Bab el-Mandeb, would join me again. My bags were literally packed and ready to go. I was really excited by the prospect. And then everything ground to a halt. At the tail-end of 2019, a small cloud had appeared on the horizon which rapidly grew till it began to block out the light all over the world. A mysterious disease that started in a city in China few of us had ever heard of. The disease was called coronavirus, and it was spreading fast. Some 1,500 NATO troops were now infected and quarantined. Exercise Cold Response was called off. Huge let-down.

To console ourselves, Stephen and I thought, 'Sod it,' and decided to fly to Iceland for a couple of days so I could run a quick marathon there and tick another one off my bucket list. And anyway, those bags were packed and waiting in the hall. Iceland was unforgettable. I ran on the incredible Diamond Beach, so called because of the large chunks of broken ice dotted like jewels on the jet-black sand. The marathon was a success and raised more much-needed charitable funds. And then we flew home. Little did I guess that it would be a very long time before I'd board a plane again. Running Dangerously – The Polar Edition was, forgive the gag, frozen indefinitely. And everyone's lives were about to change beyond all recognition.

CHAPTER 7

'YOU'RE GOING
TO DO *WHAT?*'

Andover is a fine town set in the pretty Hampshire land-scape. Nice people. A pleasant place to live. But even its biggest fans would probably concede that it's not the most exciting place to live for an extreme adventurer. After the dangerous beauty of the Bab el-Mandeb Strait and the snowy magnificence of Yukon, Andover high street pales a bit by comparison. A trip to our local Iceland doesn't quite match up to the original.

In my case, of course, that contrast always came with added baggage. As I've said, the issue of my mental health taking a turn for the worse immediately after my extreme adventures had now become a pattern, and sure enough it now surfaced yet again. On this occasion, though, many millions of people were about to face a similar situation. On 23 March 2020, a new phenomenon kicked in. One which nobody in their wildest dreams would ever have imagined they might live through. A new word entered everyone's vocabulary. Before this, 'lockdown' meant partying in a pub after closing time on a Saturday night. Now, it meant something a lot less jolly. Yet, for the first few weeks some people found it a bit of a novelty, even a sort of welcome break from the daily slog of commuting into work. But that didn't last long, and soon many folk were getting 'cabin fever', the four walls of the house closing in and becoming a prison. And we were scared too. Scared of catching this thing called coronavirus or Covid-19. People were beginning to get sick and die in large numbers and in tragic circumstances. Not just in the UK but all over the world. The whole thing quickly became dystopian, like something out of a disaster movie. Except this was something no Tom Cruise or Charlton Heston would be able to fix.

Most people had their own particular worries and stresses. Would they lose their job? Maybe even their home? How would they pay the bills and feed their kids? In my case, I worried about my daughter Evie, now living separately with her mother. When would I get to see her again apart from on Zoom? When could I give her another cuddle? And also, of course, how was I going to raise more money to send out to Djibouti? If the flow of money stopped, everything else would too. The drills, the earthmovers, the hammers and chisels and screwdrivers. The workmen would drift off to look for other work. I pictured tumbleweed blowing down the half-built corridors. Total silence apart from the desert wind blowing through the unfinished classrooms. I couldn't let that happen. How was I going to keep everything moving? What the hell was I going to do next? Think, Jordan, think.

The universe was kind. One afternoon, slouched on the sofa in the living room, I was looking back over the past few months. The places I'd been, the people I'd met. Like a sort of mental Instagram, the images flicked through my mind. Then suddenly I froze on one of them: the image of me rowing across the Gate of Tears six months before. An image striking in its simplicity. The sea and the sky. Me alone in the rowing boat. Holding an oar. But now, in my mind's eye, that oar suddenly, magically, changed its shape. Subtly, as if by CGI, that oar turned itself into a paddle. An idea took seed in my consciousness. I knew I'd found the way forward. And soon the idea even had a name: the Great British Paddle.

• • •

Among sports nuts and adventure enthusiasts, a new thrill had been taking hold. A new(-ish) water sport, called paddle-boarding. In the past decade, its popularity had been growing at a rate of knots all around the world, not least in the

UK. One reason is how easy it is for people to get into. As its name helpfully suggests, all you require is a single-bladed paddle, a special type of board and a reasonable amount of water. Unlike surfing, which it superficially resembles, you don't need to travel to the wild coasts of north Cornwall or Malibu. Almost any stretch of water will do: a river, a canal, a lake. It's just as much fun on a choppy sea or on water as flat as a mill pond. If you're searching for inner peace, you can do it on your own. If you're not, you can join a club of other enthusiasts. And in the present dire circumstances, what could be safer and more socially distanced than being on a paddleboard?

Officially, the sport is called stand-up paddleboarding (SUP). And as happens with every new craze, those addicted to it had already started vying with each other to see how far they could push this thing – holding contests, establishing new distances and so on. I started to dig a little and discovered that though several mega-journeys had already been achieved, nobody had yet paddleboarded all the way round the coast of mainland Great Britain. A circumnavigation of no less than 2,000 miles. Right then, I thought. There it is. Staring me in the face. There's the challenge. There's the adventure that's going to grab attention and enthuse people. And if I could achieve it, there's the next great dollop of money on its way out to Africa.

At that point in time, the UK's first lockdown was scheduled to lift in late May. Though everyone was yearning for the summer, foreign holidays would still be impossible. Another word, 'staycation', now entered the common vocabulary. So, a UK-based adventure had never been better timed. If the restrictions were relaxed as promised, there would soon be nothing to stop me. Till then, as always, I could start planning and plotting. Getting the word out there, waking up the media, pitching to sponsors. Then, if all went well, I'd be able to get my arse off the sofa and start training, because there was, as usual, one tiny drawback involved. When I'd set out to cross the Bab el-Mandeb Strait, I'd never rowed before in my life. Now, as I prepared to circumnavigate the entire British coast, I had to admit that I'd never been on a paddleboard at sea either. Was I daft or what? In the next couple of months plenty of well-meaning people would tell me that I was. But listening to them wasn't an option.

The Eton Harris Group, the brilliant company that had been sponsoring me for the marathons in Siberia, Yukon, Alaska and Iceland, kindly agreed to climb on the paddleboard with me and continue their support as always. This fantastic company was now joined by another: a local company in Andover called Angel Call Handling, run by the awesome Sarah and Angela. I could never have done without these amazing sponsors, because the Great British

Paddle was going to cost much more to launch than the cold-climate runs had required. The immediate basic needs were to organise a support boat for my journey and all the specialist kit that would be needed. Above all, I had to pull together a team of volunteers to cover every aspect of the intensely demanding project. My safety was a priority, so a support boat had to be considered – with a skipper, as movement by land was still relatively restricted due to the coronavirus pandemic continuing to hold the world in its grip. Then there was the media side – websites, videos, photographs and more. These were important pieces to the fundraising puzzle that needed to be in place before I set off on another world-first attempt.

But first of all, I had to train – and train harder than ever before. The Great British Paddle was going to be the biggest 'marathon' I'd ever taken on. As with the cold-climate marathons, I sought out the most prestigious experts I could find. And luckily, although paddleboarding is a fairly new water sport in the UK, such people already exist, and I signed up for a two-week course at the Water Skills Academy on the Gower Peninsula in south-west Wales. History began to repeat itself. Just as Alex Gregory had thought I was taking the piss when I climbed into the rowing boat facing the wrong way, my paddleboarding instructor Johnny Kivell immediately realised what he was dealing with. Though he never said so out loud, he clearly thought a total novice like me could simply never achieve the goal I'd set myself, a goal nobody else had yet accomplished. But Johnny is a former paratrooper, and though I obviously didn't have the technical skills, I think he recognised in me the same military discipline and determination and hoped that by some miracle these might just see me through.

The first shock was that paddleboarding is much more physically demanding than it looks. If I'd imagined that I could just turn up, climb on the board and paddle off, straight and tall, into the sunset, I was much mistaken. The first big goal was just to be able to stand up on the bloody thing. I was a bit like a baby learning to walk – it crawls across the carpet on its stomach, then on its hands and knees, then it manages a few wobbly steps before it falls flat on its face again. So there I was out on the River Wye, lying on my belly on this oversized ironing board wondering what the hell I'd taken on. This undignified posture, the paddle tucked safely under the chest, is called the 'prone position', in which you paddle with your hands like that baby splashing in its bath. From that beginning, gradually getting up onto my knees seemed like a minor miracle, and then, wonder of wonders, I staggered up onto my feet. I felt as proud as Neil Armstrong taking his first steps on the moon. One giant leap for Jordan Wylie.

For a sport that seems awesomely simple, there is an

awful lot of stuff to learn. First of all, there are two types of paddleboard – the inflatable board and the rigid or hard board. The inflatable is usually best for beginners; it's easy to carry around in a backpack, hard-wearing and less prone to damage and a good performer on most sorts of inland water. On the downside, it tends to be more susceptible to the wind, and there is the drag of having to pump it up for every ride and then deflate it at the end. The rigid board, made of foam epoxy, is a tougher workhorse used by the real pros, and it can weather rougher, windier conditions than an inflatable can handle. When the going gets tough, the solid reliability of a rigid board is what you need under your feet, and they also tend to be a lot narrower, which helps with speed. But whichever option you go for, it is necessary to choose the right size and construction of board for your height and weight.

Even the choice of paddle isn't quite straightforward. Most are adjustable to suit your height, needing to be about 6in. taller than you. The head of the paddle is called the 'blade' and comes in different widths, suitable for the conditions you'll be facing or the type of paddling you hope to be doing. It is vital to get all this right because the paddle is what drives you forward across the water. The wrong paddle would be like having the wrong engine in your car – like putting the engine of a Mini into the body of a Maserati. Just as important is the leash that connects your body to the board. It is a dead cert that you are going to fall off your board on a regular basis, and to watch it floating off out of your reach doesn't bear thinking about. The leash, which looks like a larger version of the coiled flex on an old-fashioned telephone, can be attached to you at either the ankle or waist. In both these positions, there is a quick release mechanism in case an emergency means you need to detach swiftly from the board. (Still, the ankle attachment is increasingly seen as hazardous in case the paddleboarder can't reach it for some reason, as happened in July 2021, when a man drowned because of this issue.)

For somebody like me, a novice who was undertaking a serious venture, Johnny Kivell's instruction had to go far beyond the basic stuff required for 'poodling-paddling' about on a placid lake. For the nautical marathon I was about to embark upon, I really needed to go from newbie to paddling PhD in next to no time. Not possible, of course, but Johnny got me as close as he could. And so, I tried to absorb a whole shopping list of stuff. The right paddling strokes for the different conditions – the forward stroke, the backward stroke, the push turn, the sweep turn, the reverse turn. The basics of navigation. The right clothing for different temperatures. The safety equipment necessary to carry on the board. How to interpret a weather forecast from a paddling perspective. The essentials of nutrition and water supply. First aid on the board and how to deal with an emergency. Wireless communications. Tracking and monitoring. Respecting the environment and local wildlife. Checking out necessary legalities and possible permissions. When I lay in bed at night, all this information tumbled around my brain like clothes in a dryer.

Then the scary day came when we left the relative calm of the River Wye and went out onto the sea. The Gower Peninsula is where Wales sticks its toe into the Irish Sea, and there's nothing much between that and the open Atlantic, so the waters can get pretty wild. I'd spent years on huge container ships as a maritime security guard, I'd rowed across the Bab el-Mandeb Strait in a little rowing boat, but you only realise how much the sea can move when it's more or less right under your two shaky feet. Even when it looks like a mill pond, it usually ain't. There's nearly always some little bastard of a breeze making the board tilt under you or rock you from side to side. Out on the ocean wave for the first time, some of what I thought I'd learnt I now needed to learn all over again. By this point, I'd graduated from the inflatable I'd been using on the river. Now I was on a rigid board called an ocean touring board, the 'big boy's board'. It took me three whole days to be able to stand upright, but wow, the thrill when I finally did.

Though paddleboarding is a fast-growing sport, it was still quite a small world among the serious aficionados like

Johnny and the few others who had already taken on major paddleboarding challenges. So, long before I'd released any official email about the Great British Paddle, word of mouth was out that some daft git, a total beginner none of them had ever heard of, was planning to circumnavigate Great Britain. But what was great was that despite any dropped jaws or outright guffaws, the paddleboarding clan was incredibly encouraging. Even if they felt sure that my attempt was doomed, they seemed to want to do all they could to make it a success. Unlike in a lot of sports, I found none of the competitive egotism that can be so negative and dispiriting. Even a few of the paddleboard 'champs' reached out to me with practical advice. In short, paddleboarders seemed to be a really nice bunch; maybe it was the serenity that comes from being on the water.

Thanks to them, a battalion of sponsors soon appeared, offering to donate all sorts of kit I was going to need. Not just the smaller stuff like videocams but the major elements like bad-weather clothing and even the board and paddle themselves, which came from SIC Maui and Blackfish Paddles respectively. A great guy called Gareth Stevenson, from Get On The Water UK, was a godsend with his black book of contacts. Because by now, more and more people were getting quite excited about what I was trying to do, and the news was breaking on social and mainstream media. The idea of a guy paddling round the entire British coast on an oversized ironing board had caught the imagination. Especially as it was in aid of building a school for kids in Africa. And that was exactly what I wanted. Hands going into pockets.

Of course, there's no new idea under the sun. I wasn't the first to take on a paddleboarding marathon. A few years earlier, three other paddlers had attempted to circumnavigate Great Britain. Two of these had made it from the Thames Estuary to Land's End; the third had managed nearly 1,000km but had abandoned the attempt when faced with the seas off Scotland. Two other people had triumphantly gone from Land's End to John O'Groats on the northernmost tip of Scotland, though one of these had partly used inland rivers. I was in awe of these paddle pioneers, which might sound odd considering I was attempting something much more demanding. In my head, I kept on imagining these brave folk hearing about my plans. 'Jordan *who*? And he's going to do *what*?'

By this point, it was the beginning of July, the mid-point of 2020. Great Britain, like the rest of the world, was having a hell of a year trying to deal with the worst pandemic in 100 years and the biggest crisis since the Second World War. The massive shock and upheaval of the first wave of Covid had affected everyone; some a lot more than most. But by mid-summer, the first miserable lockdown had ended, the awful death toll had dipped a little and most people were nervously poking their heads out of their burrows, coming up for air and hoping, wrongly as it would turn out, that the worst was over.

From my own personal perspective, this was my opportunity, and I had to grab it. There was literally no time to waste. I'd calculated that I might circumnavigate Great Britan in 100 days. Even if I set out tomorrow and if everything went well (a bloody great 'if'), I'd not get to Scotland much before early September, by which time autumn would be tightening its chilly grip. And I was very aware that autumn or winter in John O'Groats would be a much tougher call than the balmy climes of Andover during those seasons. Never having been great at mathematics, I didn't know that my estimate of 100 days for the total journey was a wildly over-optimistic calculation. If I had known, I might just possibly have thrown in the towel before I'd even started and found some other way of building that school in Djibouti.

• • •

So, I'd done the training. The sponsors were rolling in. The wider public was starting to sit up and take notice. But one huge piece of the jigsaw still wasn't there, and I had to put it in place fast. Without it, the Great British Paddle simply wouldn't happen. Though I'd obviously be on that paddleboard quite alone, it would also, in another sense, be pretty crowded on there. Because I would just be the public face of an adventure that would only be possible as a team effort; I needed a bunch of people who would provide me with practical, hands-on support every mile of the way, giving me the latest weather updates, organising my food and shelter, supervising my safety and a hundred other things that had to be considered. But who would they be? Where would I find them? And how quickly could it all be done?

The very next day after finishing the course in Wales, I put an ad on Facebook. Good old Facebook. However you feel about Mark Zuckerberg and his Silicon Valley buddies ruling the world, there's no arguing that FB is spectacularly useful. Within twenty-four hours, I got a message from two really awesome people who would make a massive contribution to the Great British Paddle. We did a quick Zoom call so I could expand on what I was trying to do and why, and less than a day later I found myself in their front room in Gosport, Hampshire.

I'd never been in a house like it before. It was extraordinary. But then the house was a reflection of the extraordinary couple who lived in it. Alex Alley and Paula Reid were, I soon realised, like royalty in the world of extreme adventuring. In most houses, people decorate the walls with pictures of their kids in school uniform or their animals, but Alex and Paula displayed the memorabilia of their many incredible exploits over the years. The skis Paula had used going to the South Pole. Nautical maps, oars and bits of sail from their maritime expeditions. Instead of paintings, they had framed motivational quotes about endeavour and achievement. Trees grew in pots in the kitchen. Going into that house was an adventure in itself.

In a sense, it was hard to accept that Alex and Paula ever actually lived in a house. Even harder to picture them doing the dull, ordinary things like going to Tesco or washing the car. One could only really see them halfway up a mountain or battling the winds mid-ocean. Indeed, their current project was to row the Atlantic. They were slightly wacky and totally wonderful. Instead of exchanging wedding rings, they'd given each other top-of-the-range sunglasses. Like me, their objective was to continually push at their boundaries, to break out of their comfort zones and to 'lead a life less ordinary'.

Alex Alley was in his fifties, a short, stocky guy with an amazing pedigree as a multiple world record-breaking sailor. The previous year, he'd spent seventy-six days alone on his 40ft racing yacht in an attempt to smash the record for a solo non-stop round-the-world voyage. After more than 14,500 nautical miles facing some of the roughest ocean conditions, he'd been forced to abandon the journey due to a rigging failure. But a setback like that, crushing for most folk, could never slow down a man like Alex. Within two days of his return to the UK, he was co-ordinating the rebuilding of the 90ft sailing yacht *Champagne Hippy*, which he then raced across the Atlantic, finishing seventh in a field of 170 yachts. The guy was, quite simply, amazing. A man of grit and steel.

Paula Reid was an equally impressive adventurer. She'd skied the 1,000km distance from the coast of Antarctica to the South Pole. She'd sailed round the world in the Global Challenge race. She'd cycled across twelve countries and paddled the 5,000km length of the Mekong river in southeast Asia in a dugout canoe. But Paula was even more than all that. Armed with an MSc in applied positive psychology, she had now become a pioneer in a whole new field called adventure psychology. This is a different discipline to the already well-established sports psychology which focuses on short blasts of highly intense activity over a short period of time, like a football or tennis match. By contrast, adventure psychology is about surviving, coping and thriving in variable conditions over an indeterminate period of time, like sailing round the world or being daft enough to paddleboard around Great Britain. Paula's goal was to plant and nurture the special mindset and psychological skills needed to successfully bring off these challenges. Not just for extreme adventurers like me but for people in the military or even just in high-pressured business environments. Despite my own mental health issues, when I had the idea of the Great British Paddle it hadn't crossed my mind that I might find psychological support useful. In the weeks and months to come, I would quickly discover how wrong I'd been about that. Paula Reid would prove to be the gift that kept on giving.

In that amazing house in Gosport, the three of us gelled at once. It didn't take longer than one cup of coffee to know that we 'got' one another. Instinctively, Alex and Paula understood me and where I was coming from. They were enthused and excited by the concept of the Great British Paddle and wanted to get on board. Within an hour, we'd forgotten the coffee and cracked open a bottle of champagne. Finding them was the most tremendous stroke of luck.

At once, the three of us sprang into action. There was a hell of a lot to do and sod all time to do it if we wanted – as we really needed – to benefit from as much of the never reliable British summer as possible. Alex's role would be project manager, in overall control of the myriad aspects of the Great British Paddle. It would be his task to find us a vessel to be used as my support boat, which, with his vast seagoing pedigree, he'd also skipper. This support boat would follow me throughout the journey, supplying my basic needs, such as food and shelter, as well as human company. Alex would also organise the right clothing and the necessary technical kit, as well as liaising with the other members of the team, online and land-bound, to pull together every important element of the project during the months to come. He'd also be the liaison with those punctilious folk at Guinness World Records, keeping them up to speed with the progress being made by this paddleboard beginner from Blackpool. It was a big job and would be a long one, and Alex could hardly be expected to do it for free, so he was paid a salary out of the sponsorship money that was beginning to come in. But it certainly wouldn't make him rich; he and Paula wouldn't be buying a bigger house in Gosport, not that they'd ever have wanted one.

Paula's role would be much less tangible but not a jot less valuable; she would use her skills to make sure everyone's mental health, especially mine, stayed in good shape throughout the expedition. This process began right away as Paula worked with me, hard but gently, on my pre-departure psychological preparation: clarifying my objectives, defining the meaning of both success and failure and fixing the criteria for any possible withdrawal from the project should it prove impossible to achieve. Paula had a useful phrase for all this vital prep: 'Going knowingly into the unknown.' This simply meant that though you can't predict the future, you can prepare for it. She explained how this mental prep would help me to be less stressed in situ, to be more resourceful and to make better judgements and decisions when the pressure was on. Throughout this adventure, Paula would become the shoulder to cry on, the listening ear, the soothing voice in times of stress, calmly reassuring not just me but the whole team that we had the strength within us to keep going, to stay in the game and to achieve the goal. It's in no way chauvinist or patronising to say that Paula was to become the 'mum' of the Great British Paddle, and her contribution was to be crucial.

'Captain' Alex seemed to move with the speed of light. The bubbles had hardly flattened in our champagne before he'd tracked down the all-important support boat from a friend in the Essex Marina on the River Crouch. It was a repossessed boat, which was kind of sad – somebody's lifelong dream snatched away from them – but there was no room for sentiment, so we grabbed it. It was badly in need of some very swift TLC before it hit the water again, so through my Army Cadet Force connections in Essex I organised a bunch of local volunteers to freshen up the paintwork, make it habitable and do some basic engine maintenance. As the Army Cadet family always is, they were enthusiastic, motivated and did a great job in the short time available. Alex decided to dub the boat *Coyote*, a somewhat fierce name, which, in the event, it couldn't quite live up to.

Alex had also put the word out, and in next to no time people were flocking to apply to join the support team.

Probably the most important of these was a guy called James May, who is a photographer and film-maker specialising in adventure stories. It is James's goal to use his work to inspire people with the positive benefits of extreme adventures and outdoor life. His job with us was to capture the progress of the journey and post the videos on social media and our website in order to maintain public interest over a long period and keep the pennies rolling in. We also needed video evidence to present to Guinness World Records when the time came.

James and I had an instant rapport and a lot in common. Much the same age as me, James had been in the military for fourteen years, but now he'd given up his sniper rifle for a camera. 'These days I shoot film instead of bullets,' he liked to say. As old soldiers, James and I instinctively had many of the same attitudes. No nonsense. Stop farting about. Let's do this. Those attitudes which when facing up to a really tough job are worth more than anything. On the Great British Paddle, James would become very much more than a cameraman; he could cope with pretty much anything – logistical problems, dealing with supplies, even me on an off-day.

A great woman called Katie Brooks also came on board to build the website and run it for the duration of the project. This too was a hugely important role, as the website was the prime link between us and the outside world, stoking and maintaining constant engagement with our online followers and with mainstream media. Katie's company, the wonderfully named Bear Behind, had both the facilities and the experience of charity-related work that we needed to achieve this. Throughout the weeks and months to come, it would be Katie's job to keep a 24/7 spotlight on the Great British Paddle. She also mastered the fine art of getting her hands on freebies whenever we needed them, whether it be a bed for the night, an extra piece of kit or a decent meal.

Freya Barnes joined the team as social media manager, with the similar responsibility of keeping our social channels buzzing about how the adventure was progressing and making sure our sponsors and other supporting organisations were benefiting from as much exposure as we could give them. Freya runs her own print and design business called Mye Prints, so she would also be in charge of designing and creating a collection of printed products, such as T-shirts, which would help to swell the coffers as I paddled along. We also had Stu Edmondson, like James another ex-RAF man, but we didn't hold that against him. Stu would pop in and out of the project as time allowed him, and he proved another great asset when available.

As the project evolved, several more brilliant volunteers would join us, but for the time being as we rushed to launch the Great British Paddle, this was the core team.

But what about the route? There was a simple choice. The

first option was the anti-clockwise route, turning 'left' out of Essex, heading up the North Sea coast to the tip of Scotland, then down the west coast through the Irish Sea to Land's End and back along the English Channel. The advantage of that route was that if all went to plan, I'd tackle the far north of Scotland before the really crap weather set in. The second option, the clockwise route, was the simple reverse of that. As he was an experienced sailor and my project manager, Alex Alley would decide. He was the guru on everything to do with winds and tides and all that stuff. Like Moses coming down the mountain with the Ten Commandments, what Alex decreed about everything nautical was, as far as I was concerned, written in stone. Not surprisingly, he went for the second option, the obvious logic being that the gentler seas along the southern coast in midsummer would be a far wiser training ground for a novice paddler with no more experience than a two-week beginner's course. As for the north of Scotland in winter, we'd cross those waves when we came to them.

So now I had the paddleboard, the paddle, the kit, the equipment, the sponsors, the support boat and a great bunch of people on my team. Now I just had to see if I had the balls.

On Sunday 26 July 2020, a small group of people came to the Essex Marina at Wallasea Island on the River Crouch to wave me off. Covid restrictions were still in force so there couldn't be many, but I appreciated each and every person who made the effort. Family and friends came. Some of my generous sponsors. The Army Cadet Force lads and lasses who had worked so hard to tart up the *Coyote*. And an inspirational chaplain called Pat, whom I'd met in Yukon at the start of the year. Pat's special mission is to bring spiritual or religious support to sports people at times of particular challenge and possible anxiety. I'm not especially religious, but I was really thrilled that Pat had travelled out to Essex to bless the boat, to bless me and to bless the project of building the school in Africa.

Obviously, the vibe on the quay that day was ultra-positive with a definite party atmosphere, but some of the goodbyes were difficult. My daughter, Evie, eleven years old now, never seemed fazed by the weird things her dad got up to. She was shifting imperceptibly from child into teenager, and I didn't want to miss any of that, but it would likely be at least three months before I saw her again. On top of that sadness, I had to say farewell to a lovely woman called Megan with whom I'd recently begun a relationship. I was still badly scarred from my traumatic break-up with Evie's mother a few years earlier and very cautious about dipping my toe back into those particular waters, but Megan was such a wonderful woman that I really wanted to take that risk. So, on that front at least, my extended disappearance and total focus on this new adventure wasn't well timed. But Megan had been really supportive so far, and I just hoped and prayed that she'd hang on in there.

In the past few weeks I'd also been buoyed up by and was grateful for the countless emails and texts from the many people, most of them strangers, whose imaginations had been fired by what I was trying to achieve. I treasured one in particular, from a guy called Jono Dunnett, who is a record-breaking windsurfer. He holds the round-Britain windsurf record and was the first person to complete the task too, so he knew exactly what he was talking about. 'It's going to get tough,' he'd written. 'Really tough. On so many days, you're going to want to pack the whole thing in and head home to your nice warm bed. On those days, you must keep a mantra repeating over and over in your head. The mantra is simple. STAY IN THE GAME. No matter how cold, wet, tired and miserable you are. No matter if you're in physical discomfort or even pain. Keep focused on your goal. Remember why you're putting yourself through all this. Repeat the mantra till it's hard-wired into your brain because if you don't, you may fail. Repeat it to yourself a hundred times a day. Stay in the game. Stay in the game. Stay in the game.'

And so the big moment came. It was 11.18 a.m. The *Coyote* with Captain Alex at the helm had just sailed off down the River Crouch ahead of me. Naturally, I was the focus of every eye on the marina quay. Even though it was a blow to my vanity, I thought it wise to set off on my knees rather than standing up, and I sent a silent prayer out to Pat the chaplain in the hope he might pass it on upstairs. '*Please*, don't let me fall in now!'

Gently and very, very carefully, I paddled out of the marina onto the river and towards the open sea, heading for the biggest adventure of my life. The Great British Paddle was underway. The comforting sound of cheers and applause from my friends faded away on the breeze. Despite knowing that I had my support team around me both on sea and on land, the essential loneliness of what I was about to face suddenly hit home. A man. A paddle. An oversized ironing board. And the sea itself, in all its many moods. Beautiful and dangerous. Benign and malevolent. And always, always in charge. Christ, what have you bitten off this time, Jord? More than you can chew?

CHAPTER 8

THE DEEP SOUTH

It might have been high summer, but the sea didn't seem to know that. It certainly wasn't taking a holiday, floating calmly and just enjoying the sun. Oh no. From the moment I paddled nervously out of Essex Marina it was showing me it had no intention of being an easy ride. Not that it was pushing me back, though; on the contrary there was a good strong tide pulling me down the River Crouch towards the open water. Maybe the sea was thinking, OK, let's show this silly bugger just what he's taken on.

The previous evening, in the cabin of the *Coyote*, Captain Alex and I had carefully plotted the course for the first day. The target destination was Margate, right on the south-eastern tip of Kent. Alex and film-maker James May would sail ahead of me to the open sea and the cardinal marker point, which would be the official starting line of the Great British Paddle. My first objective now was to find the *Coyote*, which was somewhere about 5km in front of me. This should have been fairly straightforward, but the sea had other ideas and I still wasn't entirely used to my new hard paddleboard. Compared to an inflatable, my 14ft SIC Okeanos ocean touring board felt much more sensitive under my body, reacting faster to changes in the waves and forcing me to adjust to different challenges with my balance. Even though I was on my knees, I was really having to concentrate totally on every movement of both board and paddle. Whenever I did risk looking around me, I saw the cosy confines of the River Crouch beginning to get ever wider, and then gradually becoming the open sea. Water, water everywhere and all of it seriously choppy.

And where was that bloody boat? At last, I spotted it way ahead of me. But the size of the waves meant that I kept losing sight of it. OMG. Supposing I actually lost the boat? Supposing the boat lost me? But eventually I got close to it – though I'd been well warned that unless I was boarding or embarking, I shouldn't get too near because the wake from the boat would affect my balance and give me something extra to deal with. But it was a great relief to see Captain Alex and James waving across the water. 'A bit too bumpy for you, Jord?' James shouted over. 'I see you're still in the praying position.'

With *Coyote* leading the way, we headed out into the Thames Estuary and the open sea. Sure enough, I soon started to see the tankers and container ships, those scary leviathans of 21st-century shipping, all around me. These waters were the nautical equivalent of London's front door, with merchant shipping from all over the globe heading into and out from one of the world's largest ports. And there was I, paddling across it. I vaguely remembered that poem about the charge of the Light Brigade but heard the words a bit differently in my head. 'Tankers to the right of him, tankers to the left of him … into the valley of Death paddled Jordan Wylie.'

And another snippet of schoolroom history came back to me. I wasn't that far from the great docks upriver at Tilbury. That was where Queen Elizabeth I had delivered her famous inspirational speech to the sailors about to embark to fight the Spanish Armada. I scanned the coastline to see if Queen Elizabeth II had turned out to do the same for me. We'd had that cosy chat at Windsor after all. But there was no sign of her. No doubt she was busy watching the 2.30 at Kempton Park.

All through that first day, the wind became increasingly strong. A wind of about 10 knots was the most a novice paddler would really want to handle, but this was easily pushing 18 knots. Christ. But, somehow, I managed to make it through the watery minefield of the Estuary. And it was now that for the first time I noticed a phenomenon which would recur constantly throughout my journey: when you lose sight of the land, you also lose the reference points which it provides and which prove to you that the paddleboard is actually moving forward – e.g. a promontory, a cliff face, a lighthouse or other buildings on the shore. Without these, it can feel like you're not going anywhere, and I always found it harder on the many days like that.

But hallelujah. Somehow by the end of the day we'd made it to Margate. I'd chalked up seven hours of paddling, all of it on my knees. When I eventually stood up to get on board the boat, my legs screamed blue murder due to the build-up of acid in the muscles and joints, an experience I'd soon learn to live with, hellish though it was. I'd covered a distance of 22km at an average speed of 4.3kmph. I soon discovered that knowing the nerdy facts and figures of what I had (or hadn't) achieved in a day was very valuable psychologically, either allowing me a small pat on the back or a large kick up the arse to do better the following morning.

'The boy done good,' said Captain Alex today. 'Not bad at all.' Not bad? The boy thought it was a bloody miracle.

•   •   •

That night on the *Coyote*, my knees and I slept like babies. But there would soon be plenty of nights when I wouldn't be allowed to sleep at all. The nights when I'd be out there on the sea, paddling all alone in the darkness. Because the Great British Paddle wasn't going to be any sort of nine-to-five job. Captain Alex may have held the title project manager, but he had taught me that the real bosses were the sea and the weather. I learnt fast that I had to do exactly what they dictated, and if I didn't, a price would be paid for my insubordination. This meant that whenever the sea and the British weather kindly offered up a 'window', you grabbed it gratefully – whether it was a warm sunny afternoon with an infinite horizon, or calm seas during the wee small hours in the pitch black when you couldn't see further than the tip of the board.

But if I'd patted myself on the back for that first paddle, the second day was a rude awakening. July or not, there was no window. The conditions just wouldn't permit any paddling at all. In a way it was good that this happened so soon, because I was going to have to accept this degree of frustration over and over and over again. This constant on–off pattern was to be one of the major psychological challenges of the expedition, but the trick of dealing with it was to try to use the downtime profitably, both by welcoming the opportunity to rest my body or by promoting the expedition to the media to attract more donations. One of the objectives of the Great British Paddle was to raise awareness of the 'Respect the Water' campaign run by the Royal National Lifeboat Institution (RNLI), whose objective was to encourage responsible water sports, including paddling. So, I found myself on BBC Radio Kent talking about these important issues.

The third day was no better, but Captain Alex, guru on everything to do with winds and tides, decreed that there would be a window that night at around 3 a.m., which, with luck, might take me from Margate to Ramsgate. It would be only my second major paddling stint and my first time on the water in the darkness. I wasn't exactly looking forward to it. I'd known it must happen, of course, but I'd not expected it quite so early in the game.

And so, at 3 a.m., having grabbed as much sleep as I could, I got out of my cosy bunk, got dressed in all the gear, slipped over the side of the *Coyote* into the water and climbed onto the paddleboard. Despite having had a nice rest for the past forty-eight hours, my knees remembered that they'd been here before and soon began to gently protest. I could hear them, of course, but I refused to listen. Though it's always important to hear what your body is telling you, there are times when you simply have to apply a mental discipline and shut your ears. And that time was now. My knees and I could do our moaning later. Right now, we had to get on with the job.

And that job was tough. Although the boat kept fairly close to me and its tiny pricks of light were an indispensable guide and comfort, I have to admit it was an eerie experience. As I've said, when you can't see land it seriously affects your sense of movement. You're paddling through the treacly dark with little feeling of forward progress. I knew at once that I was going to find night-time paddling very challenging. In the absence of daylight, even being on the open sea with nothing around you for miles can feel strangely claustrophobic, as if you are hemmed in by an endless wall of blackness. Far more so than during the day, you're aware of your solitary confinement in the world of the board. It's just this piece of epoxy beneath your feet, the paddle in your hand and whatever part of your body is hurting most at that particular moment. And the water. Because of course you're not really alone. The sea is your constant companion. Day or night, it is always alive, always moving, throwing its sudden, unexpected curveballs, demanding that you pay it your undivided attention.

Yet on that very first night-time paddle, I had it relatively easy. It was July, the dawn came early and boy was it good to see the first streaks of light appear in the eastern sky and feel the first weak warmth of the sun on my face. It was certainly just as well I didn't know then about the far bleaker nights I'd soon have to face. In the coming months, more than a few dark nights of the soul would be coming my way.

But hey, I did it. In those early hours, I notched up over 35km and made it to within reach of Ramsgate. This was good news, as was the welcome fact that I'd now left behind me the last of the dangerous shipping lanes of the Thames Estuary. The bad news was that, once again, I'd had to kneel all the way, and when I came to stand up again and board the *Coyote*, my knees threw another major tantrum. 'What are you doing to us?' I guess they were asking. 'Haven't we always done well by you, Jord? We've carried you through wars, we've supported you through marathons across both scorching deserts and thick snow. For thirty-five years, we've kept you going with nary a twinge of protest, and now you go and do this to us. How *could* you?' We clambered painfully back into my bunk and cried softly together.

•　•　•

'God, I've got the most bloody awful headache,' said James May in the cabin of the *Coyote*. 'I had it yesterday too. It's got to be the fumes from this boat.'

'Yeah, it's certainly a bit whiffy,' I agreed.

'I'm sure it's getting worse too,' James replied.

'Alex says it's fine. The boat hasn't been used for a while, that's all. It's like it's clearing its throat.'

'Maybe, but it might be me who throws up pretty soon.'

The smell of fuel was certainly pervasive. Captain Alex, who after all had sailed boats across oceans, didn't seem that bothered at first. Though the boat had been out of the water for a long while, the engine had only clocked up about 30,000 nautical miles. Surely nothing could be seriously wrong. But it soon became undeniable that the *Coyote* was a pretty sick vessel. In Ramsgate Marina, some sort of engine paramedic was summoned with his bag of tricks.

In the meantime, the weather was fine again, and I was determined to press on as planned, heading for the next rendez- vous point. Hoping that the engineer's diagnosis would be upbeat, that he'd successfully operate with a few spanners and that soon the boat would be able to catch me up, I now spent the whole day without any kind of support at all, except the food and water in my waterproof bag. I paddled off out of Ramsgate on a calm sea. My confidence on the new board was gradually building and my balance and co-ordination with the paddle were improving too. All this meant I'd also started to feel more at home on the sea. The feeling of being part of some sort of maritime community had first come to me when I started working as a security guard on the big ships all those years ago. And though being on a paddleboard was about as far from that as it was possible to get, a similar sense of belonging to that community returned to me now. Once again, I was just somebody else who lived on the water among the sailors on the merchant ships, the fishermen who trawled daily in their little boats off the Channel ports and the crews of the passenger ferries. Even like the water-skiers and jet-skiers. And this sentimental notion suddenly became very real later that day, when a small boat ran aground off the coast and lost its signal to the local coastguard. I was able to pick up the signal and relay it to them, so triggering a rescue mission.

The moment we realised that the *Coyote* wasn't going anywhere that day, James May, ever resourceful, had quickly hired a van and was now following me along the coast, as closely as the road network would allow him. Any hope of this being a temporary strategy was dashed when Captain Alex radioed to give us the engineer's diagnosis, which had been swift and certain. There was a potentially dangerous fuel leak. The boat would have to be hoisted out of the water into dry dock and the engine removed and meticulously examined to discover just what the problem was. Otherwise, it might not just be the boat that was fatally afflicted, it could be the three of us too. Blown to kingdom come. Our bodies draped over the lampposts of Ramsgate.

And so, on only the fifth day of the Great British Paddle, we'd lost the support boat, one of the most important elements in the whole expedition. The *Coyote* hadn't lived up to its name. Instead of being a strong and fearsome creature, it had turned out to be a bit of a wimp – an expensive one at that. We'd also lost Alex, at least for the time being, as he needed to remain in Ramsgate to oversee the situation with the boat. It was a cruel setback so soon in the game.

Luckily, James was a cool customer, a guy who not only stepped up to the plate in a crisis but who leapt up onto it and grabbed the controls. Obviously, there was no way whatsoever that I could continue without some form of logistical support. Equally obviously, we just didn't have the funds to simply hire another boat and carry on regardless. The clear answer, the only answer, was that James would hire some permanent kind of transport and continue to follow me by road. Far from ideal, but we were stuck.

We put out word on social media, hoping by some miracle for something that could provide as many of the facilities of the *Coyote* as we could get: primarily accommodation; a place to eat and to rest our weary heads. Something like a 3–4 berth motorhome would have been the dream, but we would consider almost anything except a horse and cart. Failing that, James and I were going to be needing beds for the night for the foreseeable future. When it became clear that the *Coyote* was permanently disabled, it was agreed that Captain Alex would go home to Gosport and run the project remotely from there, providing us with daily weather updates and all the other necessary information as we went along. So, Plan B was quickly conceived and implemented, but there's no denying the loss of the boat was a massive blow. The air above Ramsgate that day crackled with the sort of language you'd not want to use in front of your mum.

But not for a moment did I think of packing it in. Jono Dunnett's mantra kept buzzing round my brain. The boat was out of the game alright, but I was staying in it. And then guess what? If there is a God of paddleboarders, he/she now decided to shine his/her light down upon me. The next day as I set out towards Dover, the weather glorious yet again, I managed to stand up for the very first time. I felt like I'd just conquered Mount Everest.

•   •   •

'There'll be bluebirds over the white cliffs of Dover,' sang dear old Vera Lynn. I'm not that big on birds, not the feathered kind anyway, so I wouldn't have known a bluebird if it shat on me directly from above. But there were certainly a thousand gulls hovering over the huge ferries moving in and out of the Port of Dover. It seemed to be my destiny in this life to be surrounded by gigantic ships.

It was another glorious summer morning. The great walls

of the white cliffs soared above me as I waited patiently to cross the harbour as soon as there was a gap in the ferry traffic. If the Thames Estuary had been like Oxford Street, this was Piccadilly Circus and every bit as dodgy. I suppose I could have made my way across the harbour mouth without asking permission, but I wanted to follow best practice on this expedition, so I radioed the port authorities for formal clearance to do so. 'You may cross now, Mr Wylie,' said the voice eventually. 'We wish you all the very best with your challenge.'

'Roger that, thank you, sir,' I replied, the soldier in me never far from the surface. A bit of courtesy costs nothing.

This exchange reminded me yet again just how many people were now aware of the Great British Paddle. Katie Brooks and Freya Barnes, the team members in charge of our website and social media presence, were clearly doing a great job. On my long journey along the south coast, it would become more and more apparent what a big wave of support and encouragement was flooding out towards me. Sometimes I'd actually meet those supporters on a beach or glimpse them waving at me from a clifftop. At the worst moments of loneliness to come, they would be an invaluable comfort. Now, as I paddled cautiously across Dover Harbour, I could see the passengers lining the rails of the ships, eager to set sail for their summer hols in the Med, delighted to be free of lockdown after the long months of isolation. I wondered if any of them had been following me online and maybe recognised me now. 'Here, it's him,' I imagined somebody saying. 'That bloke who's paddling all the way round Britain. Total nutter, but you've gotta hand it to him, ain't cha?'

But not everyone who came out to greet me had been on the website or followed me on social media. There was a whole other bunch of folk who would pop up from time to time, regardless of the weather. I never knew when to expect them or how long they might hang around, but whenever they did it really did my heart good. The sight of a dolphin breaking up through the sea, the sunlight and water shimmering on its skin, must be one of the most beautiful sights you can experience on this earth. There's just nothing like it, I promise you. And if you're lucky enough to get two, three, four or more of them, the magic is off the scale. They're such amazingly sociable animals, intelligent and sensitive. And curious too. They'd simply come to see who this guy was and what the hell he was doing. Every time it happened, I felt privileged. In moments like that, all the sadness and pain in the world seemed far away. And whatever sadness still hung around in the dark corners of me seemed to vanish too. I was on a paddleboard in the middle of a blue summer sea in the company of these beautiful creatures. It just didn't get much better than this.

And on this hangs a tale. Not long after I left the *Coyote* on that fifth morning, I made an interesting but slightly scary discovery. When I fumbled in my kit for my medication, I couldn't find them. Shit. Those little helpers were supposed to keep me on an even keel – a highly appropriate analogy for a bloke on a paddleboard. By now they'd be in the dry dock, God knows where, to which the damn boat had been taken. I knew that the odd missed day was no big deal because the effect of the meds was cumulative, so I wasn't too worried at this point. I told myself that when I hit the next town, I could try to get a new prescription sent through to a local pharmacy. It wouldn't be a problem; I'd had to do that one day during the marathon back in Yukon, though it had cost me an arm and a leg, so my carelessness now needn't be the end of the world. But then I asked myself a question: supposing you don't do that, Jord? Supposing you just stop taking them and go cold turkey? Supposing the Great British Paddle is all the therapy you really need? The sea, the sun, the fresh air, the dolphins and that sense of purpose pushing you on every single day. Remembering your 'why'. Thinking about that school now slowly rising in Djibouti. And besides, you can always talk to Paula Reid via the comms if you feel low.

The more I thought about it, the more it seemed like a plan. A potentially life-changing plan. My spirit soared at the thought of it. 'OK, Jord,' I said to myself. 'Let's do it. Let's just see what happens.'

And as I paddled onwards from Dover, I allowed myself to imagine that the dolphins racing ahead of me through the water were validating my decision. As if they were saying, 'Come on, you're going to be just fine.'

CHAPTER 9

THE KINDNESS OF
STRANGERS

'I have always depended on the kindness of strangers.' I think that's a line from a famous play, though I can't remember what it's called. But that was certainly going to be the case throughout the Great British Paddle. Thanks mostly to social media, people seemed to materialise by magic to offer the help that was needed at any particular time. This was a real blessing because in losing the support boat the dangers and difficulties of the expedition had notched up quite a bit. I'd always known that what I planned to do made me vulnerable in many ways, but that was now tenfold.

After losing the *Coyote*, James May and I would spend nearly sixty days without a support boat and therefore an automatic place to sleep. In high summer with the weather tolerable it wasn't a total nightmare; James, with typical efficiency, had quickly organised a tent so we could sleep on the beach if needed and eat basic campfire food, just like we'd both done in the military. But now Katie really mastered the online networking and cold-calling thing, and offers of an evening meal and a bed for the night came flooding in. There were so many of these, sometimes five or six offers for the same night in the same town or village, that Katie had to resort to making a spreadsheet to keep track of them all. Some came from private houses, others from local B&Bs and hotels. The private offers never wanted any sort of payment, but often even the hotels and B&Bs didn't either; they were just enthusiastic about the project and wanted to support it. Snoring in a nice comfy bed with a good meal inside you was a hell of a lot more preferable to lying in a tent on a lumpy beach, trying to keep the sand out of your bum crack.

The result was that, in this respect at least, the loss of the boat had a definite silver lining. Never quite knowing whom we'd meet that day or where we'd sleep almost became the best part of the adventure. We met all sorts of great people: young folk, noisy families and elderly couples. We stayed in simple homes where money was clearly an issue as well as in some definitely posh gaffs. The generosity was amazing, and no matter how tired and aching I was at the end of a long day on the water, James and I would always try to give something back. Like providing the cabaret, for example – telling them tales of our lives in the services, of fighting the Somali pi-rates, of climbing expeditions, of working on TV shows and all that jazz. And listening too. Everyone in this life has a tale to tell; everybody has their own joys and sorrows, triumphs and disasters, and I had long since discovered that you can learn something, however small, from hearing those stories.

But this wasn't a jolly holiday; this was a serious challenge, and discipline could never be entirely relaxed. So, no matter how late the evening, I'd often need to be up and back on the water at an early hour. Captain Alex remained in constant contact, his weather reports always the arbiter of what I'd try to achieve that day. Through them, I slowly began to learn so much more about the winds and the tides and all the erratic behaviour of the sea. Though some of this knowledge was a bit scary, it was increasingly vital now that I no longer had the boat, neither as a sanctuary nor as a lifeboat in the event of serious trouble. Being blown out to sea and lost for ever was not the way I wanted to go.

The loss of the boat also intensified that inevitable feel-ing of loneliness on the paddleboard. I knew of course that James was following me along the coast in the van. We were in touch by radio, but most of the time I couldn't actually see him. Some days, the reality of that could be challenging. By now I'd come to realise that though all my positive talk about pushing out boundaries and broadening horizons was totally valid, it was equally true that my essential existence had now shrunk down to a short plank of epoxy resin on a tiny patch of water. I now lived in the world of the paddleboard.

So, let me try to describe this world I now inhabited. My home-from-home on the ocean wave. Allow me to show you around. Almost all the 'furnishings', attached either to the board or to my body, were not surprisingly about safety. Since I'd almost certainly end up in the drink now and again, my primary lifesaver was my personal flotation device (PFD), a highly sophisticated form of lifejacket with bright green lights on its front to signal that I was OK. The PFD had pouches all over it to hold various bits of kit. A whistle. A knife, a fork and a spoon to eat the light meals stored in a waterproof bag securely attached to the surface of the board. A multi-tool implement for use in various tricky situations, e.g. cutting away a fishing line or other flotsam and jetsam that might have got entangled with the fin on the board.

To keep me in touch with the help I might need, I also carried a personal location beacon (PLB), a device registered beforehand with local rescue centres so they could find me quickly in case of trouble, and an Icom radio tuned to the emergency Channel 16 used by all the port authorities and seagoing crafts. I also had a strobe light like those used on top of police cars and a hand-held flare, to help the rescue services pinpoint my position after I'd called them out. I had an Iridium tracker and even a satellite phone too. And, obviously, a mobile phone in a waterproof bag, which depending on the signal strength often worked well up to 20 miles offshore. All the important numbers were stored on this phone: the port authorities, the coastguard and my family and friends. It was vital to always carry spare batteries for most of this equipment. Nobody wants to die for want of a Duracell. So, these state-of-the-art gadgets were all my new best friends. My lifelines connecting me to safety and security. Every day before I set off on the board, I checked them all over as carefully as I'd once checked my rifle and my radio before heading into the dangerous corners of the Iraqi desert.

But dangerous territory isn't the exclusive preserve of the Middle East; the county of Kent can be a bit dodgy as well. 'Cannon to the right of them, cannon to the left of them … into the valley of Death.' Blah, blah, blah. That poem came back to me once again as I headed westwards from Dover towards Folkestone with those dolphins still leading the way. The south coast of Britain isn't just golden beaches with ice-cream vans and women in bikinis, and I was now heading into definitely dangerous waters. Not whirlpools or rocks or stuff like that but big beefy blokes with guns firing in my direction even though they were on my side.

I knew the Ministry of Defence firing range at Hythe well, as I'd trained there often when I was in the military. The guns had been going 'bang, bang' there for over 150 years. With live ammo too, no dummy bullets or anything like that. The ranges are constantly active throughout the year, and the area is highly restricted most of the time, with red flags flying to warn the public away. The restricted area includes the foreshore, so I had to apply for formal permission to enter and pass through it. They don't really have time for paddle-boarders and other troublesome civilians, so they decree exactly when, and for how long, you might cross their waters without having your head shot off. In my case, I was given a window between 4 a.m. and 8 a.m., when all their sharp-shooters would be tucked up in bed with their teddy bears. It wasn't ideal. Nor was the tide in my favour, so it took longer than expected to travel across their waters. I kept looking at my watch. Twenty minutes left. Shit. I now wished I'd stuck a white flag on the end of the board. Fifteen minutes left. I remembered some of the beginners I'd trained with years ago; not every soldier is a natural with a gun, and some of them couldn't have hit a cow's arse with a banjo. I prayed that no plucky new recruit was at that very moment levelling his sights at me. Ten minutes left. I moved that paddle like a mad man. I made it with eight minutes to spare. Phew.

Still, it was a pretty good day, notching up over 37km and getting a bit more company from the local marine inhabitants. I spotted four dolphins, nine seals, five jellyfish and two crabs. The next thing of interest I noticed was an old man's willy – yes, you read that correctly! Without knowing of its existence, I'd found myself passing close to a nudist beach. An elderly gent was on the sands taking his constitutional, the morning paper under his arm, his man boobs bouncing as he went along. And that wasn't all that was bouncing. I waved in a friendly way, expecting the same in return. But he must have seen the camera gear I was carrying and assumed I was a press photographer conducting a fearless exposé of geriatric naturism and determined to put his boobs on Page 3 of *The Sun*. Angrily, he started shouting and gesticulating for me to go away. No problem, mate. I'm out of here. I really didn't want to see your old todger anyway.

But another major obstacle lay ahead. Dungeness is a vast headland of shingled beach that sticks out into the English Channel like Pinocchio's nose. On its tip is the ugly pimple of a nuclear power station. A few houses are scattered here and there, but it's a bleak place, desolate even. Pancake flat like some English version of a desert, its atmosphere is a million miles from the jolly beaches of Folkestone and Hastings not too far away. Yet Dungeness has a strange sort of beauty that many artists have tried to capture, including the painter and film-maker Derek Jarman, who lived and died here in an isolated cottage. It's also an important nature reserve, a haven for huge numbers of wildlife, and many species live here that cannot be found anywhere else in the country.

From my point of view, the great spit of Dungeness was to be a real challenge; my first major headland of the Great British Paddle. The currents are known to be tricky and the winds ill-tempered. On top of that was something the local fishermen call 'the boil': a patch of sea where the waste pipes from the power station pump hot water into the sea. The wildlife love this warm bath, a nice change from the chilly English sea; personally, I didn't much fancy bathing in water from a nuclear reactor. So, Dungeness seemed likely to test my novice paddleboard skills to the very limit, and it was my great good fortune that a highly experienced paddleboarder and mariner called Mark Rose, who lives locally, had contacted me on social media and offered to pilot me round this tricky bump in the road. Mark is a total water sports nut who runs the nearby Varne Watersports Club, and, with his wife Chris, he had taken his board to exotic locations like Vietnam, eager to experience the joy of the sport on every possible type of water. Mark and Chris, generous in every way, had given James and me a great meal and a bed the previous night. Mark knew Dungeness and its idiosyncrasies like the back of his hand and now helped to plot a route around it, explaining to me how the sea reacts to the intrusion of this long spit of land and how in turn the paddleboard might react to the water movements at certain awkward points of the journey. Though my teacher was impeccable, his pupil wasn't quite, and this was to be the first time on the expedition that a rogue wave caught me unawares and turfed me into the drink. Well, it had to happen sooner or later. Annoyingly, I lost a new pair of shades and a really cool cap. And of course a bit of dignity. Mark must have seen what a newbie paddler I was, but he never said anything to diminish me, and for that I was grateful. Sure enough, with his company and encouragement, I made it round Pinocchio's Nose. Once again, I had depended on the kindness of strangers and they'd come through big time. And at least nobody was firing at me or waving their willy.

But I was soon to learn that though 99 per cent of people I'd encounter on the Great British Paddle were welcoming, generous and supportive, there were a few who weren't. Often these were local fishermen who seemed to get irritated by anyone who wasn't a fisherman too. While I understood that the sea was their livelihood, some of them had the attitude that it belonged to them and that nobody else had any right to be anywhere near it. These encounters were usually on beaches, from which their fishing lines were cast many metres out into the water. To avoid these lines, I'd need to go much further away from the shore than I wanted to. On one occasion when we knew this problem might arise, James had motored ahead to ask politely for permission for me to pass, more out of courtesy than anything else. But these guys, grumpy gits muttering under their breath, refused any compromise, which meant I ended up paddling under their fishing lines flat on my stomach, which was exhausting and far from easy. This miserable bunch didn't deserve our politeness; they deserved two fingers. But I managed to behave like a gentleman despite silently hoping they'd catch nothing more that day than a few dead goldfish flushed into the sea down someone's loo.

Luckily, that wasn't true of all the fishermen. Some of them were as curious about the expedition as anyone else, and as helpful too. I soon learnt that they were a valuable source of information about everything to do with local waters, about the winds and tides and where the riskiest places were. Some of these guys were real old salts, their faces weather-beaten into leather by the sun and the wind. Old men of the sea. And sure enough, they always knew where the shipwrecks were. It might have been the *Mary Ann* which sank in 1827 or the *Valiant* which had been torpedoed by the Germans in 1943. I made a mental note to avoid becoming the *Jordan Wylie* who went down in August 2020.

There was one thing these fishermen – whether nice or not

so nice, whether English or Welsh, Irish or Scottish – nearly always told you. That 'their' headland was the toughest in the whole UK. And that I was going to have a real bitch of a time getting round it. As I paddled on westwards from Dungeness, that phrase didn't seem so empty. Because coming my way was the grandaddy of them all, the image from a million postcards: the iconic Beachy Head.

Nobody had ever told me about Beachy Head. I knew what it was, of course: a massive chalk headland somewhere on the south coast, which, like the white cliffs of Dover, was a major tourist destination. But somehow I'd never known that Beachy Head was also a destination for another type of visitor – those whose depression, hopelessness or grief had reached the point where life no longer seemed worth living. Over the years, many hundreds of these people had taken that leap into oblivion I'd once come so close to myself.

These days, there's a team of volunteer chaplains who patrol the area day and night looking for potential suicide victims and reaching out to them, sometimes literally. There is a phone box on the clifftop, surrounded by signs for Samaritans in the hope that in their worst moment desperate people might just make the call and be persuaded back from the edge. Or maybe just the sight of that phone box might trigger them to use their mobile and call someone who cares for them. Someone who would, as my own mum had done on that distant day, know from their voice that something was terribly wrong.

But now, on this beautiful morning as I paddled towards that ghost-white 500ft wall, my own mental health seemed better than ever. I'd done without the pills for a few days now and had felt no side-effects whatever. I'd actually called my GP in Andover to let him know what had happened, and he'd told me firmly that I was playing with fire and that a cold-turkey withdrawal could be a serious mistake. 'But I'm feeling great,' I replied. 'Just great.'

'Maybe, but your life isn't exactly normal right now, Jordan,' he said. 'You're doing this big thing and it's not quite the real world, is it?'

'Well, it's the real world to me,' I replied. 'Totally, 100 per cent real. I'm not dreaming this.'

It was that old battle, of course, the one we all come up against now and again. My head telling me that he might just possibly be right and that I was being a bloody fool, but my heart telling me something else entirely. As is often the case in these matters, my heart was winning hands down. Because there I was, back on my ironing board after a good night's sleep. The August sky was cloudless, the swell of the sea was gentle and seductive. A few seals had already stuck their snouts above the surface to say good morning. I was doing something I really wanted to do, for a cause that meant everything to me. There were now thousands of people enthusiastically following my daily progress online, not to mention all the folk along the route who'd already been so generous with help, advice and hospitality. So why wouldn't I feel as great as I did? How many people, working endless days from home during the pandemic or otherwise squashed onto buses and trains on their way to tedious jobs, wouldn't envy me right now? Almost as every hour passed, I became more and more convinced that I no longer needed those damn pills. In my imagination, I pictured the thousands of tablets I'd consumed till now floating away on the water behind me like flotsam and jetsam, as I paddled on into a pill-free future. My spirits soared at the thought.

Yet at the same time, in the back of my mind I was conscious that it might well have been a very different kettle of fish if I had stopped taking my medication while stuck inside the four walls of my home in Andover. It is really important to note that these were exceptional circumstances, and it is absolutely crucial to consult a doctor before stopping any medication. But out on the sea, by now I felt increasingly convinced that this adventure, like the others before it, was the only treatment I needed. The difference this time was that the feeling was so much more powerful and liberating – and I knew there was a name for it too, as other people had spoken and written about it. What was happening to me on this glorious morning off Beachy Head was called 'blue therapy': the power of water to calm and heal the spirit.

Lots has now been said about blue therapy. Scholarly articles by some clever people and research projects by universities. It's always been well known that plenty of exercise and fresh air have positive benefits on physical and mental health. But in recent times there's been increasing awareness that the contemplation of water can bring a particular sense of calm and well-being. It's an instant escape from the noise, pressure and stress of the modern world. Anyone with a tank of tropical fish in their front room can tell you that, as can anyone who goes swimming at their local baths. Even just the simple sight of it seems to do the trick. Sitting on a park bench looking at a lake. Strolling on the beach. Paddling in the shallows. There's something elemental about watching sunlight glitter on the water or the waves breaking onto the sand that resonates with something primitive inside us. Helping to give us perspective on our troubles. Replacing negative thoughts with positive ones. Reconnecting us with our environment, which has become ever more difficult in modern life and ever more important.

But actually being *on* the water travelling across its surface seems to amplify that sense of well-being many times over. Breathing less polluted air, the breeze on your face and the sun (hopefully) on your back. Hence the lure of rowing, surf-ing, water-skiing and now paddleboarding. It feels so good to learn more about the various forces of nature, how the tides and the winds work, how all this affects the movement of the water underneath you. And because this demands your total concentration, your everyday world drifts away, taking its worries with it, leaving just you and the elements. Most people find this hugely therapeutic. Like a magical opportu-nity to elevate your mood. Like rebooting yourself.

During summer 2020, when I was doing the Great British Paddle, huge numbers of people discovered this for them-selves. Trapped inside four walls by the first lockdown, many people felt their mental health take a serious hit, and maybe for the first time they realised just how vital some degree of connection with the natural world actually is. The daily hour of permitted exercise had become a lifesaver. And many of those lucky enough to live near the sea, a river or an inland lake took swift advantage of that good fortune. Paddleboard retailers saw increased sales of several hundred per cent, often running out of stock. Blue therapy was here to stay.

It was certainly working well for me as I headed towards Beachy Head on that perfect August morning. But a very careful assessment had been necessary before I'd set out. One of the constant, and serious, challenges of the expedition was whenever I had no 'exit point' from the water onto a beach, usually due to a long wall of cliffs. So it was always vital to carefully check the winds and the tides beforehand in order not to be blown onto the rocks. Thankfully, yet again, another stranger magically appeared to guide me. Sarah Thornley was a lovely lady and became a great friend too; she is a highly experienced paddleboarder who writes for paddlesport magazines and runs a major industry news outlet called SUPJunkie. She knew every inch of the waters below Beachy Head and got me round without incident. I will always remember the vision of that great chalkface towering over me with its pretty lighthouse beneath and the seals and dolphins popping up out of the waves. That day, I covered 51km in a paddle of no less than thirteen hours. I was tired alright, but I felt bloody fantastic, almost believing that nothing could go wrong. But I was mistaken about that. A problem was brewing that could scupper the whole project.

CHAPTER 10

THE LITTLEHAMPTON LOUT

'**Y**ou should probably get that looked at, mate,' the young RNLI lifeguard said as he looked at the blood oozing from the big graze on my leg.

'It's nothing much. It'll be fine,' I replied, keen to carry on. And that's what I really thought. Just a graze. It was an error that would cost me dearly in the weeks to come.

He was a teenage kid on a jet-ski in the water off Littlehampton, just to the west of Worthing. A lout who thought it would be a laugh to buzz a guy on a paddleboard and tip him into the drink. And talking of drink, I suspect he had enough beers in him to be charged with whatever is the maritime equivalent of dangerous driving. There was a group of them, whopping and yelling and behaving like five-year-olds. But this particular little shit was the worst. Fancied himself as cock of the walk. Totally self-centred, with little regard for the effects of his behaviour on other people. When he clocked me, I became a challenge. I think it was because all my gear and cameras made him think I was some sort of professional water sports guard whose job it was to spoil the fun for the likes of him and his mates. So, he headed his jet-ski straight at me, coming so close I was toppled into the water. In his tipsy state, he might easily have misjudged the distance and killed me.

But once wasn't enough for him. He turned the jet-ski around and came in for a second go, his stupid mates cheering him on. By this point, a rip tide had pushed me right up against one of the long stone groynes that snaked out from the beach into the sea. On the kid's second charge, I fell in again, losing my water bottle and my sunglasses. But this time I got something worse than bruised dignity. Draped in barnacles and seaweed, the groyne looked harmless enough, and when I grazed my shin against its rough surface I didn't think much of it. But the barnacles were razor sharp, and so was the pain.

The lifeguard had seen what was happening and now came over to give the little sod a finger-wagging, but that was about it. I totally support the lifeguards and the fantastic work they do in saving lives around our coasts, but I still think they let this guy off way too lightly. I could see in the kid's face that he didn't give a shit and would probably behave just as stupidly tomorrow. I'd like to have grabbed him by the scruff of the neck and given him a piece of my mind, liberally sprinkled with unprintable words. Of course, you can't do that any more or you get charged with assault. Quite rightly, I know, because physical violence only breeds more violence and rarely solves anything much; it just sticks in my craw that the assault he perpetrated against me went essentially unpunished, and he was likely to do the same to the next paddler that came along. It was an assault which was to cause me many weeks of discomfort and pain and potentially a very serious medical condition. It could very easily have sunk the Great British Paddle.

It's easy to say, 'Kids will be kids' or 'He didn't really mean any harm' or 'I'm sure he'd be gutted if he knew about your leg.' All of which may be true – but it's also true that the direct result of his behaviour came perilously close to ending the expedition. And that would have meant that donations would stop coming in, which in turn would have meant the money would stop going out to Djibouti, the building work would cease, the workmen would all drift away and a school of 250 children would not be built – at least not yet, and, who knows, maybe never. I'd really like that kid to know about that and to understand that negative actions have negative consequences, even if we don't necessarily intend those consequences. And I'd like him to know that the world doesn't centre around himself but is filled with other people to whom, if he is to grow up into a civilised human being, he owes a degree of duty and care.

The Littlehampton Lout, as he became known within our team, was the personification of what worries me about some of our younger generation. As I'm only in my mid-thirties, I know I'm a bit premature in railing against 'young people today' like some old codger. I know too that I'm on very shaky ground, as my own teenage years weren't exactly saintly. As I wrote earlier, I was the class clown, the boy who threw away his education and only lived for the ringing of the bell at half past three so he could go and play football. And maybe if I was young and lived in Littlehampton in 2020, I'd have been out on a jet-ski too. But I honestly don't believe I'd ever have been someone who was so self-absorbed that I had no respect for other people or their safety and well-being. And sad to say, I do often see this self-absorption in young people these days, although thankfully not in all.

For many years now, I've been going round schools giving talks to pupils, including to my own old school in Blackpool. I tell them the story of my life, how crap I was academically but how joining the military, learning its values and then finding my niche in maritime security had given me a sense of identity and that I could achieve whatever I put my mind to. Naturally, they're also gagging to hear about fighting the Somali pirates, being on *Hunted* and completing extreme adventures around the world. But what concerns me is how obsessed so many of them are with the most trivial aspects of the stuff I've done, like what celebrities I might have bumped into. Have I ever met Kim Kardashian or Justin Bieber?

I find this infinitely depressing, especially when I see it seeding in the younger generations. Being the national ambassador for the Army Cadet Force is a passion for me precisely because it does its best to fight back against this sort of thing. It's an amazing organisation with the aim of helping young people to recognise and develop their skills and talents, to open their eyes to the wider world in a positive and compassionate way and to learn to appreciate the deep satisfaction that comes from focusing on other people as well as on ourselves. In the Army Cadet Force, I've encountered some fantastic young people with massive potential, and it's been a huge pleasure to share my own story with them and to demonstrate that anyone can eventually make something useful of themselves even if, as I did, you take a few wrong turns along the way and lose your path for a while.

Sadly, we're living in an age which not only makes it difficult to get that message across but which actively undermines it. Every landmark invention in human history brings positives and negatives; it's not the thing itself but how it is used. The printing press, the gun, the motor car, the aeroplane and now social media; it's always the same. I'm as much into social media as anyone else. Without it, fundraising for the Great British Paddle would have been almost impossible. It's Facebook, Instagram and YouTube which have oiled the wheels of all my extreme adventures, letting me reach out to people to ask for their support, both financial and practical, and it's through those same channels that supporters have given me so much encouragement. So I ain't knocking social media. BUT (and it's a really big 'but', triple-underlined and floodlit) it's getting ever clearer that it's doing considerable harm, especially to the younger generation, whose lives now seem to be ruled by it. Thankfully, most people have become aware of the most alarming aspects of this; the dodgy sexual stuff and the vicious bullying which can shatter mental well-being and even lead to self-harm and suicide. But there are other aspects too, less dramatic and more subtle but just as worrying.

I'm not sure quite how to label it. Trivialisation might be the nearest word. Dumbing-down maybe. Or just an obsessive interest in stuff that has little value. Like the endless selfies. The photoshopping of our own images, our tiny human flaws airbrushed out so we can somehow make ourselves more 'acceptable' to others (whatever that means). The expectation that the world should take notice of us even when there is no special reason why the world should do that. When I go round the schools talking to the kids, I often ask that age-old question: 'So, what do you want to be when you grow up?' Once upon a time, back in the Dark Ages of my own childhood, the answers might have been a train driver, a doctor, a nurse, a teacher, a hairdresser. These days, nine times out of ten, it'll be a YouTuber or a social media influencer or just 'a celebrity'. I remember putting the question to one seemingly bright teenage boy. 'I'd like to be famous,' he replied.

'For what?' I asked.

'I don't know. Just famous really.'

'But you have to be famous *for* something,' I said.

'Do you?' he replied, as if the thought had never crossed his mind.

'Yep. Like being the first to climb some mountain or breaking a speed record or getting a No. 1 hit or discovering the cure for some disease. That sort of stuff.'

'OK. I didn't know that.'

Of course, the sad fact is that he was probably right and I was wrong. If that boy grows up into a good-looking guy, if he buffs his pecs and biceps in the gym, if he somehow gets himself onto something like *Love Island* then he will indeed be famous. Even for a short time. And he will make money. But for anything of real substance? I think not. And what will he do when his five minutes of fame passes? What will he have left then? Apart from the pecs and the biceps and, hopefully, a bit of dosh in the bank which may not last too long, even if he hasn't already spent it on girls, booze, drugs and holidays in Ibiza.

I care so much about this because of my personal history. Those years when I seemed to get all my own values badly screwed up and which ultimately led to me becoming a man who had really lost his way. Maybe all this has its roots in the politics of the 1980s and '90s, the 'loadsa money' era when greed suddenly became 'good', there was 'no such thing as society' and it became not just morally acceptable but actually laudable to put yourself before other people. Such a contrast with the values of my parents' generation, who'd grown up with stories of the sacrifices their own parents had made during World War Two. I'm not saying they were saints – I'm sure they danced, drank and shagged just as much as today's youngsters do – but they knew that the world can be a very dark place indeed, and possessing that knowledge gave them substance as people. I think the word is gravitas.

So when I meet many of today's young folk, I worry a lot when I see a lack of that substance. I want to tell them that what really matters isn't how many followers you've got on Twitter, not how you look on Instagram or that your pecs are bigger than Katie Price's boobs. It's all about recognising your talents, breaking free of your comfort zone, pushing out of your boundaries and making yourself into the very best

LEFT Me and little Ibrahim on the day we first met out on the Horn of Africa, where a promise was made. © Stephen McGrath

BELOW The familiar sight of refugees passing through Djibouti from Somalia heading for Yemen. © Stephen McGrath

LEFT Training with double Olympic champion Alex Gregory at Henley-on-Thames. © Stephen McGrath

BELOW The Solent waters off Southampton were a great training ground with lots of marine traffic and changing tides. © Stephen McGrath

A visit to Djibouti to check on the school's progress. © Stephen McGrath

Be safe, be secure, be alert: wise words of advice for heading out into pirate-infested waters.
© Stephen McGrath

Mission accomplished: the mandatory end of expedition shot in front of Ras Sayan mountain and its famous shark-fin peak.
© Stephen McGrath

Deep into avalanche territory in Alaska before we had to terminate our run and head back to Yukon. © Sally Orange

A refreshing dip at Diamond Beach in Iceland was a once-in-a-lifetime opportunity that had to be taken.
© Stephen McGrath

Me and Sally Orange dressed as Disney's *Frozen* characters Kristoff and Elsa at the Siberian Ice Half Marathon. Author's collection

Here pictured during my two weeks' training before I set off. Training and remote support from Johnny Kivell and the Water Skills Academy was priceless. © James May

Army cadets from the Essex Army Cadet Force helping to prepare *Coyote* for action. © James May

Paula, James, me and Alex before deploying from Essex Marina on Day 1 of the Great British Paddle. Author's collection

After you, sir… Waiting patiently to cross the Thames Estuary on Day 1 was a taste of things to come. © James May

Sarah and Angela from Angel Call Handling visiting me at Land's End.
© James May

It was always great to see the incredible volunteers from the RNLI and independent lifeboat stations like Hamble, pictured here.
© James May

The wonderful Bluetits female open-water swim club provided morale and support.
© James May

Now you see me; now you don't. Navigating my way through the Inner Hebrides, Scotland.
© Alfie Marsh

Me, Alfie, Tori and Daz at Kilmore Quay, Ireland, waiting for another weather window.
© Alfie Marsh

Adventure psychologist Paula Reid proved a valuable asset throughout the expedition.
© Alex Alley

The postcard-picturesque Tobermory on the Isle of Mull. © Alfie Marsh

Winter sunsets on the west coast of Scotland were simply majestic. © Alfie Marsh

The west coast of Scotland in winter was beautiful and brutal in equal measure. © Alfie Marsh

Conquering Cape Wrath after attacking it for a week is a day I will never forget. © Alfie Marsh

Mia, me, Alfie and Max as we depart Scrabster Harbour in Scotland and head home for Christmas Day. Author's collection

Me and Ibrahim nearly three years later at the new school. The smiles say it all. Author's collection

It was a privilege to spend
a week with these children.
Author's collection

The first intake of pupils in their new uniforms
on Day 1 at the school. Author's collection

Christmas with Evie was the perfect end to an incredible five months of adventure.
Author's collection

person you can be. That way, you stand a far greater chance of being happy and also of bringing happiness to the people around you.

That's why, almost as soon as I first saw the site at As Eyla in Djibouti, I was determined to build the school for Ibrahim and all the others. At the same time, I had another idea. I promised myself that as soon as the school was up and running, I was going to bring a bunch of British schoolkids out there to see the way other children and young people live, in a place without the advantages most of them have been able to take for granted, just in the way I had myself a long time back. If and when it happens, it won't be in a schoolteacher, waggy-finger sort of way but just in the hope that they might quietly absorb their own good fortune in this world compared to so many others. Most important of all, I hope it might broaden their horizons, engage their interest and make them want to contribute something to people and places way outside their normal world of smart phones and social media profiles – and in doing so, help them grow up in every sense of the word.

•   •   •

Sadly, as my journey went on, I came across quite a few Littlehampton Louts. After Beachy Head, the Solent was my next big challenge along the southern coast of England. The Solent was yet another maritime equivalent of Piccadilly Circus: a dangerous combination of the huge car ferries plying between Portsmouth and Southampton to the Isle of Wight, the usual container ships heading out into the Channel and an absolute maelstrom of speed boats and other pleasure craft. Naturally, the professional sailors did everything by the book, but the amateur ones could be a total nightmare. Once again, there were people on boats who weren't even sober, let alone competent. Once again, that blinkered selfishness and careless disrespect for other people was in evidence all around me. That attitude of 'I do what I want because it is my human right to do so.'

Thankfully, what often happens just as you're totally hacked off with the rest of the human race is that your original faith is suddenly restored. It turned out that I wasn't going to have to cross that scary Solent all alone among the nutters. Once again, the kindness of others kicked in. A great friend I had met during my maritime security days, Dr Risto Talas, was one of the generous donors who had been following me online. He is a senior lecturer on maritime risks and also a former underwriter on war risks within Lloyd's of London. Now, he and his lovely wife Lindsey offered themselves and their boat, the beautiful *Black Magic*, to escort me across the dodgiest strip of the Solent, the hectic channel between

Portsmouth and the Isle of Wight. I also had the same kind offer from the Hamble Lifeboat station, one of those incredible independent stations run entirely by volunteers who give up their free time to keep the waters safe for everyone, even the half-pissed idiots on glitzy motor yachts. But in the end, it was Dr Risto and Lindsey who guided me over, like a nautical version of the lollipop ladies on school crossings.

Things were a bit less frenetic in the western Solent, beyond the ferry routes and around the quieter landscape of Lymington and Christchurch. Still plenty of other paddle-boarders though, who came out to paddle alongside me for a while and then wave me off on my solo journey. Throughout the expedition, I loved it when people came out to meet me, as it took the edge off the sense of loneliness that was always there to some extent. There were some days when I was quite content with no other company but the odd dolphin or seal, but there were also days when I wasn't. Even though James was still following me in the van along the coast and we'd nearly always rendezvous in the evenings, the long hours on the board could be tough.

It wasn't long before I met yet another secular saint. I was approaching Boscombe, near Bournemouth. For most of the day, I'd been struggling against an adverse wind, and I was knackered. And though it had been a warm August day, the evening was drawing in and I was getting chilly and hungry. I wasn't sure exactly where on the road James was, so I'd come out of the water for a short rest on the beach. As I dragged myself up the shore, this old lady appeared from inside a beach hut. Her name was Catherine, she said. 'Would you like a marshmallow, dear?'

'A marshmallow?' I replied, 'Um, yeah, why not?' I tried to remember when I'd last eaten a marshmallow. Probably around the age of eight.

'I've been watching you for ages,' she said. 'I thought you looked a bit miserable in that wind, so I put the kettle on when I saw you heading in.'

And hey, that marshmallow turned out to be delicious, as did the second one and as did the hot chocolate Catherine brought me too.

She was ninety, she said, but she loved her little beach hut more than anywhere in the world. She'd never heard of the Great British Paddle, so I told her all about it and the reason for doing it. She said that was just great and that I mustn't give up whatever the wind – I must keep on going. Catherine was one of that generation I've been talking about, the generation with a bit more gravitas than the generations which have come after it. She had still been a child during World War Two but was old enough to remember its deprivations and the sacrifices every single person had had to make. Maybe it was the memories of all that which seemed to make this old lady so glad to be alive and determined to make the most of every day. I hope and pray that if I'm lucky enough to live to a great age, I'll have even a quarter of her spirit. Released at last from the long months of lockdown, she came down to her beach hut to enjoy the blue therapy of looking at the sea and reaching out with interest, enthusiasm and encouragement to whoever came her way. And tempting them with marshmallows.

CHAPTER 11

'CAN'T YOU JUST PATCH ME UP, DOC?'

It was still summer. A pretty good summer too, as if the universe was trying to make up for the months of misery everyone had just gone through. The beaches were still crowded – far too much so in the opinion of the media and of the authorities desperately trying to keep a lid on Covid. There was plenty of eye candy sunning itself on the sands, which helped to keep me cheerful, and I was still feeling great without the medication. And, as always, lots of paddleboarders would come out and join me for a while. I'd now notched up about 400km and donations to the Great British Paddle were coming in steadily.

Unfortunately, there still wasn't enough money in the kitty to pay for the hire of a new support boat at the going commercial rate. So, until some seriously rich and angelic donor appeared, wearing wings and a halo, James and I struggled along as best we could; me on the water, James on the road. But it was often a hit-and-miss business. Selfishly, the main road network didn't always hug the line of the coast, so James would often find himself bumping down single-track lanes to get as near as he possibly could to where I was going to come ashore. And in remoter spots, the comms equipment didn't always function well, so arranging that evening's rendezvous was often far from easy. 'So, where the hell are you?'

'What d'you mean? More like where the hell are *you*?'

But we had a great relationship, so these little tensions rarely lasted for long. The nights we had to sleep in the van weren't too bad. As former soldiers, both of us had endured much worse billets than this. And as anyone who's ever been camping knows, if somebody is a serial farter you've just got to take it on the chin. Luckily, we were still inundated with constant offers of accommodation. One night we'd be squashed into somebody's spare room or a tent in the garden, and the next we'd be in quite a chic little hotel with posh toiletries in the bathroom, which we tried not to nick as that seemed a bit evil in the circumstances. But whatever the digs, the welcome was always the same.

In glorious weather, I paddled past Bournemouth and Poole with its spectacular natural harbour. Past the beautiful Studland Bay, which I later discovered is yet another nudist beach – though this time, thank God, there wasn't a todger to be seen. And then to Swanage, a pretty little resort, where we were kindly put up at The White Horse. On a late summer evening with a pint in our hands, we couldn't have wished for a better place to be.

It was just as well I'd had such a good night, because I was about to enter one of the most challenging parts of the Great British Paddle. As I've said, Captain Alex and I had agreed that the clockwise route heading west along the Channel coast was the sensible route for a novice paddler to take. That was the theory, anyway. In practice, it wasn't quite so cut and dried. Now, from Swanage, I was about to travel along the iconic Jurassic Coast of southern Britain. A stretch of about 90 miles of towering cliff coastline with almost no exit points along its length. For much of this section, I'd be totally solo and under a hot sun.

But wow, it was certainly spectacular. Great undulating walls of chalk and limestone rising sheer from the sea. Over the millennia, the gradual erosion of these cliffs slowly revealed their geological history, and the Jurassic Coast is now a UNESCO World Heritage Site. It wasn't hard to picture the odd brontosaurus ambling along the clifftops. But nowadays, it is just a wonderful spectrum of seabirds soaring above the water or banking lazily on the thermals. Not that many people were to be seen apart from at the tourist traps of Durdle Door and Lulworth Cove, which were crammed not just to the water's edge but also in the sea. I steered well clear of them but unfortunately not clear of an SAS patrol of vicious jellyfish, which got me when I had a break and let my legs dangle in the water. Luckily, it was the other leg from the one badly grazed in the incident with the Littlehampton Lout. But that wasn't much compensation because that seemingly trivial injury had now mushroomed into something quite serious.

As I said, it had seemed nothing more than a graze, but I'd ignored the coastguard's advice to get it looked at. Typical Jordan. Ex-soldier. Tough guy. Anyway, I thought, the sea water would actually be good for it. Big mistake. The sea water along that beautiful coast is frequently polluted with all sorts of horrors, including faeces, and some of that shit had headed straight for my wound. Over the next three to four days, the initial mild discomfort had turned into something more painful. The leg and ankle had started swelling up, and since my legs took so much of the strain, the business of paddleboarding gradually became more and more difficult.

Most of the time, being determined and focused on your goals is a major plus, a necessity even. But there are times when it's just bloody stupid. The trick, of course, is to know the difference, and on this occasion I'd got it spectacularly wrong. For more than a week after Littlehampton, I'd tried to forget the increasing discomfort, obsessed with keeping going at all costs. But now, as I reached Weymouth, I could no longer pretend not to have a serious problem. Help came from a kind physio called Elaine, a paddleboarder who'd been following the adventure online. She took one look and knew at once that a dollop of muscle rub wouldn't make a blind bit of difference. 'The leg's infected, Jordan,' she said. 'You've got to go to A&E. And fast.'

'Oh, come on, I just don't have time for that,' I replied.

'If you don't go to A&E right now, you soon won't be going anywhere else.'

At the hospital, they took about ten seconds to diagnose cellulitis, a nasty disease of the blood vessels that needs swift treatment with antibiotics. If I'd taken the coastguard's advice, I might have avoided this. Lesson learnt.

'The main thing, Mr Wylie, is to keep the leg as dry as possible,' the A&E doctor said. I had to laugh. I told him what I was doing. He didn't laugh at all, just looked a bit too serious for my liking. How the hell was I going to keep my leg dry? It would've been easier to fly to the moon. 'I think you probably need to postpone that for a while, Mr Wylie.'

'No way,' I replied. 'Can't you just patch me up, doc?' I think that was a line I remembered from some old western starring John Wayne as the wounded gunfighter who's still got the last shootout to do.

With a long sigh, the doc did just that. I was given

waterproof dressings and headed back to the sea. But the dressings never worked that well; water was always determined to get in somehow. For the next few weeks, I'd suffer a long process of partial recovery followed by partial setback. I'd even have to visit a couple more A&E departments along the way. There would be more pills, stronger pills. The leg would get a little bit better, then seem to get a bit worse again. Gradually, I learnt to live with the situation and to keep going, but it was far from ideal. I'm going to donate a free copy of this book to the public library in Littlehampton in the hope that The Lout might happen to read it one day.

The timing of this drama wasn't brilliant, because Weymouth was the gateway to yet another big hurdle. I certainly hadn't become blasé about the hazards of headlands despite having got round Dungeness and Beachy Head, which was just as well because Portland Bill was going to be a right bastard and no mistake. This wasn't because of any fearsome, towering cliffs. Like Dungeness, Portland Bill is a fairly undramatic promontory of almost flat land that looks harmless enough. But the dangers here were similar to those at Dungeness: the intrusion of the land into the sea and the effects that has on the winds and the tides. Other paddleboarders had given me a red warning about going round the notorious Portland Bill.

At first, all was deceptively well. That morning, Cal and

Rusty, two of my old army mates, turned up bearing a breakfast from McDonald's. Maybe not the healthiest start to the day but bloody good all the same. I was even seen off by Sammy, the famous Weymouth seal, who popped his nose up right at my designated starting point. Sammy had recently become something of a local celebrity, an outgoing chap who enjoyed giving slippery hugs to swimmers and who was even known to hitch rides on paddleboards just for the fun of it. Sammy stared at me for ten solid minutes, no doubt weighing up his chances of a lift. Normally, I'd have been happy to have Sammy riding shotgun for a while, but he really was one fat boy and paddling was tough enough without 1,000lb of extra weight, so I was glad when he just gave me a wave with his flipper before he submerged himself again. Nice of him to turn up though.

Like so much of this stunning coast, Portland Bill was a beautiful sight on a clear blue morning. The passage from Weymouth Harbour out towards the tip of the promontory was surprisingly smooth and gave me more confidence than was wise. At the very tip of Portland Bill, by the historic lighthouse and right above the sea, is a weird formation called Pulpit Rock, so-called because it strongly resembles a huge bible resting against the lectern of a pulpit. It is easy to imagine Charlton Heston as Moses in *The Ten Commandments*, standing there in billowing robes with his hair blowing in the wind as lightning flashes and thunder rolls, issuing heavenly instructions to mankind. Maybe commandments like 'Thou shalt not be daft enough to paddleboard around Britain.' Because, as everyone had warned me, once I was on the far side of Portland Bill, things were suddenly very different.

Seemingly out of nowhere, the tide quickly became dangerously strong. At once, I had to drop to my knees for my own safety. On top of that, a sea fog started to roll in. I now urgently needed to utilise everything I'd learnt from Johnny Kivell at the Water Skills Academy. About fine-tuning my balancing, about which paddle strokes to use, in fact every sodding trick in the book to keep me on my board and well away from being catapulted into the rocks, against which the waves were throwing themselves in dramatic plumes of milk-white spray. Out of the mist, an RNLI boat appeared close by and called out to check if I was OK. Paradoxically, they advised me to go closer into the land, the very opposite of what I'd been striving for. It seemed there were as many rocks below the water as above it, and these would have the positive benefit of reducing the worst impact of the tides. Clever stuff. I took their advice and made it round Portland Bill. I got back up off my knees. My heart rate dropped. The sweat dried on my body. But it was a very sharp reminder that you must never underestimate the power of the sea, never imagine you know all its ways, never tell yourself you can handle whatever it throws at you. The sea was the real project manager of the Great British Paddle. It always was, always would be. I'd forget that at my peril.

Westwards from the Bill, the water gradually quietened down. Another group of friends and their families now appeared on the beach, armed with a few Cokes and some snacks. People were always so kind. But, almost as soon as they'd waved me off again, I found myself facing a challenge of a totally different sort.

Coming towards me now was one of the most famous images from the picture postcards. Chesil Beach is a seemingly endless strip of shingle about 30km long that stretches from the west of Portland to near Bridport. Its most iconic section lies just beyond Portland, where the beach separates the open sea from a large tidal lagoon so there is water on both its sides. This makes the beach look like a narrow causeway rolling away to a hazy horizon between two different seas, a road to infinity.

Its biodiversity makes it an important haven for wildlife, and that's why public access is restricted during the mating season in high summer. This makes Chesil Beach entirely different from other places along the south coast. There are no bikinis, lilos or jet-skis here. No stripey umbrellas or ice-cream vans. Not even any nudists. Instead, it is a place where the elements rule. Sea, sky, shingle and nothing else, the earth stripped back to the barest essentials. Apart from the cackling of the sea birds, the only sound is of the wind and the waves breaking onto the pebbles, some as big as a fist, some as small as garden peas. The absence of people can almost make it feel like some post-apocalyptic movie in which the world's population has been wiped out, leaving only a few survivors. And on this day, one of those survivors was me. Despite its great beauty, there's an undoubted sense of sadness about Chesil Beach, and unexpectedly it was here maybe more than anywhere else that the Great British Paddle became psychologically challenging.

Part of it was that phenomenon I've described before in which the loss of markers such as buildings or a lighthouse or even just the unchanging contours of the landscape would rob me of any sense of the paddleboard moving forward. This issue kicked in big time on the 30km Chesil Beach. I was paddling as fast as possible but nothing around me seemed to alter. Sea, sky and shingle. Nothing else. No trees, no hills. I almost wished the Littlehampton Lout would make an appearance.

Apart from the damn leg, tightly wrapped in its supposedly waterproof dressings, and the ongoing aching of my knees, I was physically pretty good. By this point, I hardly ever thought about the tiny risk of another epileptic seizure, the possibility that had so freaked out my GP. I still took it seriously, though, and luckily I'd not forgotten the medication for that ailment and carried it with me 24/7. And mentally, after well over a month on the board, I was still feeling absolutely fine. As far as I was concerned, the blue therapy was working like a charm.

But that journey along Chesil Beach was definitely a wobble, even if a short-lived one. As a rule, I was relaxed about being on my own; I loved company and could be a party boy when the need arose, but I could just as easily do without it and often even sought out solitude as an antidote to the busy world in which most of us now live. But today there wasn't even a phone signal to let me contact James, still following along the coast in the van, though he was still able to track my position by satellite. There was just something about the loneliness of the beach that affected me. I remembered too the sad film *On Chesil Beach* starring Saoirse Ronan, about a troubled honeymoon couple whose happiness finally fell apart on that beach and led them to take different paths – a decision they would regret for the rest of their lives. I'd done that myself, of course. Taken the wrong road. Lost my perspective. Hurt people. Sacrificed the family life I'd held so dear.

And now, as I paddled along past that never-ending ribbon of shingle for six long hours, those faces from my life came to keep me company. My parents. Laura, my ex-partner and still good friend. Megan, the lovely woman I'd only just got into a relationship with and of whom I had high hopes. Above all, my daughter. I even had imaginary conversations with them, saying things I'd meant to in the past, words that should have been spoken and hadn't always been. It helped. I remembered that I wasn't alone in my life. So many people are, but I wasn't one of them. Count your blessings, Jordan. After a while, I put some karaoke into my headphones and combatted the beautiful melancholy of Chesil Beach by belting out the old favourites. I wondered what the gulls above me or the dragonflies nesting among the grasses of the beach were thinking. I didn't care. I'd sing if I wanted to.

•   •   •

It was called Storm Kyle: the first of a couple of tempests that were to batter Britain in the summer of 2020. We knew it was coming, and we knew it was going to be big. So big that Captain Alex had come down to Bridport to discuss the best way forward. But we quickly realised there was no way forward. None at all, unless I'd suddenly developed a suicide wish. My leg was still in quite a bad way. The antibiotics hadn't really kicked in yet and every minute on the paddleboard was delaying its healing. Apart from the approaching storm, a serious rest was needed, which went against every instinct I had. I'd just notched up 500km. I couldn't stop now.

But neither the leg nor Storm Kyle was listening. It's a weird thing, this new habit of giving people's names to weather events. And often such inappropriate names too. Why Kyle? I know somebody called Kyle; he's a nice guy, not remotely tempestuous. How about Storm Evil? Storm Dracula? Storm Massive Pain in the Arse? That sort of thing. Anyway, the forecast for Kyle was pretty dystopian. Winds like the hounds of hell. Massive seas. Thunder and lightning. It was biblical stuff. It looked like I would be going nowhere for quite a while.

But though James and I wouldn't be going anywhere, we'd be doing that somewhere very nice indeed. One of those following me online was a man called Major Charles Fowle, now retired, who'd been an officer in the King's Royal Hussars, my old regiment. Our years in the army hadn't coincided, but he'd been carefully tracking my journey, and now he invited us to come and stay for as long as necessary at his house in the Seaton area, near the mouth of the River Axe, which divides Dorset from Devon. Seaton was a pretty little resort with a magnificent beach, but there was little chance of embarking from that beach out into the wide waters of Lyme Bay. The skies over the south-west of England were darkening by the hour, and we were more than happy to accept Major Fowle's invitation. Since he was a major and talked a lot posher than either me or James, we pitched up at his place in our humble van feeling pretty confident that this might be a passable billet.

But wow, that was an understatement. It wasn't just a house but a country estate, with tennis courts, a swimming pool and every other conceivable comfort. Charles was in his fifties now and the officer commanding the Devon Yeomanry. Living in his perfect house was a bit like being in the officers' mess (not that ex-trooper Wylie had ever really known what that was like). And though we'd never met, the brotherhood of the regiment never dies. The food was wonderful, the drink plentiful and the camaraderie first class. There was nothing Major Charles liked more than sharing his memories of his days in the regiment. After dinner, over a glass of port or two, all our stories tumbled out, many of them funny, some of them sad. The places we'd been, the people we'd known, some of whom we'd lost but would never forget. And I always liked to spout the old motto 'Better by far, a King's Royal Hussar'.

These days, Major Charles is heavily involved in the removal of landmines in Africa and had seen their tragic results on many of the children in war zones, so he was very empathic with the reason for the Great British Paddle. His charming wife Caroline didn't seem to mind in the least that her peace and quiet had suddenly been invaded by a pair of slightly scruffy NCOs, one of them with a leg wrapped in slightly unsavoury dressings. For nearly a week, this wonderful couple wined and dined us, gave us shelter from the storm and even did our laundry, all of which allowed us to make hefty savings on our outgoings.

Storm Kyle, when it arrived, fulfilled its pre-publicity. It was a corker, with 70mph gales and torrents of rain. So, we didn't get around much, and living like kings, we tried to convince ourselves we didn't want to. But of course that wasn't true. However seductive the generous hospitality of Major Charles and Caroline Fowle, I was still champing at the bit to get back on the waves.

It was at times like this that Paula Reid, the adventure psychologist, was totally invaluable. Talking online to her was always like getting a vitamin injection of positivity. When the negative stuff raised its ugly head, she'd show me a way of re-evaluating the circumstances and finding a kernel of positive thinking, however small, that would let me 're-frame' them and view them differently. This lengthy sojourn at Seaton was a prime example of Paula's 'reframing', because this enforced lay-off was exactly what my leg needed, giving it the chance to rest, stay bone-dry and kick-start the healing process.

The messages of support still poured in every day from the huge numbers of people who were following me online. Lots of people encouraging me to stick with it and stay in the game. That phrase again. It was already my mantra – especially when I was tired, lonely, a bit hungry and my nuts were frozen inside my wetsuit. I guess it's the thought every extreme adventurer clings on to when the going is rough. When the obstacles seem insurmountable. When you've really had enough of this crap. When you feel very small and very human. No doubt adventurers in previous times had exactly the same thought, even if it was phrased in more flowery language. 'Thou shalt endeavour to do one's best.' 'Gird your loins and battle on regardless!' That sort of gung-ho thing.

Then, suddenly, a possible weather window opened up. Captain Alex told us that it would probably happen at first light the next morning. Saying a grateful goodbye to Major Charles and Caroline and their soft, comfy beds, we drove off that evening and spent the night in the van close to the beach, in order to grasp the opportunity if and when it came. And it did. I only managed less than three hours, all of it on my knees, but I made it round a deceptively challenging headland at Beer Head and clocked up another 8km down towards Branscombe. Not much, just one of Jono Dunnett's 'small hops', but another step towards my goal and that was all that mattered.

The late August weather continued to be distinctly ropey, and I pitied all those poor holidaymakers who had looked forward to their breaks for so long and were now being washed out in the resorts along the Devon coast. An ice cream or a hot dog really ain't much compensation for being blown to buggery on a rain-swept English prom. St Tropez or Marbella it definitely wasn't. But we were pleased to get to meet the amazing crew of Sidmouth Lifeboat, all of them volunteers. All around Britain, these independent lifeboat stations go on saving lives every year. Trained by the RNLI but not funded by them, these indie stations have been hit hard by Covid. In 2020, most Brits opted for a staycation, so the resorts were even fuller than usual. Yet during the lockdown, the charity shops on which these organisations rely so heavily for income had been shut. It was a double whammy. But still those awesome volunteers sat there ready at a moment's notice to go out to sea to rescue people, often from avoidable situations they'd brought on themselves. It was the operational policy of the Great British Paddle to always check in and inform lifeboat and other rescue stations when we were about to enter their territory. We'd brief them on our kit and equipment, our assessment of the risk and the plan for our passage through their waters. We'd also ask for any specific local advice they could provide, which often can't be found in any book or website. As we say in the military, time spent in reconnaissance is seldom wasted.

For the time being, it seemed like many more small hops would be the order of the day. The next morning, even though tide and wind were dead against me, I managed another 22km down to Budleigh Salterton. Along the way, Mother Nature decided to throw in another one of her surprises. I was looking up at the majestic cliff scenery when all of a sudden part of it disintegrated before my eyes and collapsed into the sea like shit off a shovel. Landslides were something the team would increasingly have to plan for as summer morphed into autumn and winter. After heavy rainfall such as that brought by Storm Kyle, these were always going to be a serious risk, and I'd always need to steer a wide berth of these great walls of chalk – after having stood invincible for a thousand years or more, they could in certain conditions vanish in less than a minute. Despite the pleasures of blue therapy, I didn't really fancy being buried at sea.

But Mother Nature still hadn't finished with her surprises. As soon as Storm Kyle had moved on to create havoc elsewhere, its brother, Storm Francis, came hurrying along trying to catch its coat-tails. Once again Major Charles came to the rescue, and we drove back to Seaton to sit it out. Once again,

70mph winds and 90mm of rain hit the west and south-west of Britain. Roads and railway lines were blocked. Firefighters had to rescue campers, caravanners and the odd stray dog. But at least Storm Francis, unlike his thug of a brother, had the good manners not to hang around. The worst was soon over, the waves calmed down and the holidaymakers ventured out from the hotels and B&Bs. It even felt like summer again, and soon the distances were notching up as I made my way along the so-called 'English Riviera'. Not far off 600km now and over £6,500 in donations so far.

To make the best of the weather windows, I had to do a couple of night paddles – never my favourite thing. As I've said previously, in the dark unless there's some moonlight you can't see what's coming your way, and it was so easy for a rogue wave to catch me out and turf me into the water. One time that happened, I'd just spoken to my dad and he'd jokingly said to be aware of the sharks. Suddenly, I could hear that scary theme from *Jaws* pulsing in my head and I'd never got out of the water so fast. I didn't want some old lady dog walker coming across my half-chewed remains mixed in with the flotsam and seaweed the next morning.

But squeamish readers really should stop here and skip to the next paragraph. That same night, off Teignmouth in Devon, I found myself in the water once again, this time of necessity. After thirty-four days of the Great British Paddle,

I was forced to perform an act I'd been pleased to avoid so far. That's right: my first poo at sea. I wasn't proud, but nature really was calling. By now, I'd got quite used to performing my No. 1s while on the board. Sometimes, if the sea was flat calm, it was even fairly easy to get the old man out and pee into the water. But if it was at all choppy, it was very tricky to do that and keep my balance on the board. In those circumstances, I'd just have to let it go into the neoprene suit, a sensation which is not as unpleasant as you might imagine, especially in chilly weather. But now, in the dark with no beach or other exit point, it was No. 2 calling. Only, not calling but screaming. I tried to hold it in for as long as I could till I got to shore, but it wasn't having any of that. Getting the bum out of a neoprene suit is not an easy matter, and nor is the business of emptying the bowel with your legs moving at the same time so you don't sink. But the job, so to speak, was accomplished, and fortunately I was far out at sea next to rocky headland, away from any tourist beaches. Once again, though, I could hear that music in my head. The tailfin coming at me unseen through the darkness. Then the huge teeth sinking into my arse, making the poo completely unnecessary. When I got back onto the board, the light from my headlamp illuminated what I'd just produced as it drifted past the board. Not a clip I'd be posting online.

• • •

Despite the week of rest in Major Charles's stately home, my damn leg was still in trouble; it just wasn't healing properly. Another long drive to A&E, this time in Plymouth. Another great nurse, this time called Ally, yet again ex-military and an adventurer. I began to think that every A&E in the country must be staffed by such amazing women. The bad news was that cellulitis was still present; the infection was not notably worse, but it was far from better either. The dressings simply were not able to keep it dry. Standing all day on a paddleboard with the English Channel washing all over it was the worst thing possible. Not only did the leg get wet but the infection was going downwards into my ankles and feet, making them swell up. James, never one to accept any sort of defeat, scoured Plymouth high and low till he tracked down some super-special medical dressings in the hope of making a difference. But even those weren't a miracle cure. The miracle cure would've been a fortnight in the Maldives with my leg up.

But on we went. Moving west along Devon and into Cornwall, there were plenty more headlands and estuaries to be negotiated along the beautiful coastline. Brixham, Dartmouth, Salcombe. Still, the weather was erratic; blue skies morphing to funereal clouds then back again. By now, we'd made an important discovery about weather forecasting which would become a slight issue throughout the Great British Paddle. Captain Alex, back in Gosport, remained our daily forecaster, his role in the project still invaluable. As Alex had sailed across the world, nobody could have been a more intelligent reader of the winds and tides. And yet. It often happened that the weather predicted on the meteorological charts, and which Alex warned us to expect, simply didn't materialise in reality. Alex might say that the weather tomorrow would be dire and impossible to paddle, yet from where we were standing it was absolutely fine. Or vice versa. Being ex-soldiers, programmed to obey our senior officer, James and I found it awkward to argue with the captain. Then again, what was the point of sitting on the beach while the sea was a sheet of blue glass, all because Alex's forecast predicted the worst weather since the pages of *Moby Dick*? It was a dilemma, and one which led to occasional tensions within our otherwise harmonious team. I learnt that the weather forecasts never took into account the topography of the land, which was very important as depending on which way the wind was blowing, I was sometimes able to use the cliff lines as cover and cheat the wind, so to speak. As with so many other aspects of the expedition, it was often a question of taking a calculated risk by gathering the information, analysing and discussing it, then agreeing on the course of action. On a gig like this, sticking to these military-based principles was always a huge advantage.

And despite the storms and the sodding leg, I still felt the constant magic of what we were doing. Almost every day there would be some image which I knew would stay with me for a long time. Seeing a magnificent pod of a dozen dolphins breaking through the surface close to the board just as the sun came up. Crossing the vast harbour at Plymouth past a huge warship and dozens of other examples of Britain's naval heritage. The stunning sight of a double rainbow. Who wouldn't want to be alive at moments such as those?

And still, more great people kept coming our way, offering us meals and accommodation, generosity and friendship. At Plymouth, we met a nice man called Marcus Cronin, a teacher and a fervent member of the local SUP community. Marcus treated us to a meal in a local hotel and then, quite unexpectedly, gave us something very much more. When we met local people, they'd want to hear all about us and the expedition, and so we'd usually find ourselves doing all the talking. That happened this time too, but something about Marcus made us want to know his story. When it came, it was heartbreaking: the story of his late wife Caroline, another water sports fanatic, who had died of a brain tumour way too young seven years before. Knowing that her illness was terminal, Caroline had told her husband that she wanted two things before she passed away: to get married and to have a child. And miraculously, this amazing woman had managed to do both.

It may sound daft to give a name to an inanimate object, but if people could do it with boats, why not a paddleboard? So I decided that name would be *Caroline*, and as soon as it was possible that's the name I painted on it. Not just in memory of a brave and feisty lady who loved the sea but also in respect for this fine man who had shown such quiet courage and strength.

• • •

West of Plymouth, along the jagged coast of Cornwall, I began to feel a distinctly different chop to the sea beneath the board. The shelter of the English Channel, relative at the best of times, was now giving way to the influence of the Atlantic Ocean. The waters became choppier, the winds more mischievous. One day I spent a whole nine hours down on my knees until they cried for mercy. It was like being in a washing machine for which somebody had chosen the wrong cycle; on and on and on it went. It was one of my toughest days yet. The side winds were dreadful. I ended up in the drink four or five times and I threw up at one point due to sheer exhaustion. One of those days when even the sight of a dolphin wouldn't have cheered me up. Not that there were any dolphins; they all thought bugger this and stayed below the surface. Another day I only managed 17km in seven hours. But the south Cornish coast was spectacularly beautiful. A mixture of creeks, coves and cliffs, pretty little ports and harbours and country houses half-hidden among the trees. This was the world-famous romantic setting of Daphne du Maurier's novels like *Rebecca* and *Frenchman's Creek*. Pirates and smugglers and mysterious gothic mansions and all that stuff. For a paddleboarder it wasn't romantic but seriously challenging. The rugged coastline was full of traps which rendered my usual strategies useless. If I tried to avoid the worst headwinds by clinging close to the cliffs, a tangle of unpredictable undercurrents would pull and push at the board, as if trying to throw me off. Making progress was a daily battle. At least I didn't encounter the ghost of Rebecca rising from the deep.

By now, there was no doubt that my body was really feeling the effects of having paddled for nearly 800km from the Essex Marina. The damaged leg and the red-raw knees were the worst of it, but now in general my whole body was thinking, 'Hey, whoa, enough.' My hands were starting to blister, my lower legs were cramping all the time. At only thirty-five, I was beginning to feel about ninety.

And yet all the time, in those small hops, I was getting closer to Land's End, which would mark the completion of the first phase of the Great British Paddle. But the biggest obstacle to reaching it still lay ahead of me: Lizard Point, the most southerly tip of mainland Britain. The approach to The Lizard was the clearest evidence yet that the Atlantic Ocean was now making its presence felt. The swell grew more formidable as I paddled towards this iconic landscape. Cornwall is an ancient kingdom of myths and magic, of King Arthur and Camelot; however, contrary to popular belief, The Lizard isn't named after some legendary creature but possibly derives from the Cornish word 'lezou', meaning 'headland'. Not quite as romantic. Whatever the truth of it, it's a wild and exposed place which makes you feel that you're right on the very edge of the world and that the wind, if it had a mind to, might blow you over the edge and into the devil's cauldron. Getting round The Lizard meant paddling for 8 long miles without any exit point along the shoreline. It was a real test of my focus and endurance. There's a small tourist restaurant on the cliffs, and I was no doubt photographed on a hundred phones by people enjoying a Cornish pasty and a pint of local beer. It was little compensation.

Land's End was now no more than a day's paddle away, but I almost began to feel that it didn't want me and was pushing me away. Covering those last miles seemed to get harder all the time. The penultimate stage was a night paddle of almost 40km, nearly nine hours in the dark, most of it on my knees. It was also bloody freezing; my coldest night yet and an ominous portent of things to come. From Mullion, past Porthleven, St Michael's Mount and Mousehole to Penberth Cove. The trip was made bearable by two kayakers from Porthleven called Ian and Shaun, who came out to escort and guide me across their local waters. Not just bearable but memorable for a lesson learnt. When Shaun had last taken a pee from his kayak, he'd forgotten to zip up the flies of his drysuit. Easily done, as every man knows. But later his kayak had been hit by a rogue wave and capsized. The water gushed into his drysuit via the open fly, filled it up in no time and very nearly drowned him. It might be vaguely amusing, but it also wasn't at all. Certainly not the nicest way to go, dying because you'd needed a pee.

Oddly enough, despite the cold of that night, a daft bit of me wanted to push onwards from Penberth and complete the remaining kilometres to Land's End, but I knew deep down that was a mistake. I'd paddled nearly 70km in the past twenty-four hours. I needed rest; I needed energy. Besides, I knew that at Land's End, the TV cameras would be waiting for me. Not that I'm vain or anything, but I wanted to look respectable and motivated, not like the knackered, shivering, half-drowned rat I really was.

• • •

As I paddled towards the headland, all I could hear were the usual sounds of the sea crashing against the rocks and the gulls and gannets whirling round in the sky above me. Then, suddenly, something else caught my ear. At first I couldn't think what it was, and then I realised it was the sound of people. People making a lot of noise. For a moment, I wondered if some rowdy pleasure boat had crept up on me from behind, but no, it wasn't that. I glanced up towards the cliffs and saw a big crowd perched along the edge. Waving, cheering, camera phones flashing, the works. I'd expected that reaching Land's End would be a bit emotional, but I'd never imagined anything like this. I felt my throat tighten up. Wow, wow, wow.

It had been forty-five days since I left the Essex Marina. I'd now chalked up 900km on my circumnavigation of Great Britain. I had an infected leg, tortured kneecaps, blistered hands and aches and pains almost everywhere else. I'd been stung by jellyfish and harangued by grumpy fishermen and elderly nudists. I'd been thrown off the board into a cold sea and at times had felt an overwhelming loneliness out there in the pitch dark. And I knew there was probably much more of all that to come, maybe even worse. But the support of an amazing team, the goodwill of so many people along the way and the encouragement from the huge numbers of people who were now tracking me online made all that bearable. However rough things had been and might get in the weeks and months ahead, there was no way I'd ever pack this in. Come hell or high water, or even both of those together, I knew that I would always stay in the game.

And now, there was Land's End rising above me in the early autumn sunshine and a bloody great crowd roaring down. All along the south coast, Stu Edmondson had been acting as a sort of runner for the expedition, helping us out in various ways as and when we needed additional help. His usual job was working with hammerhead sharks in the Pacific, so nothing much could faze him. I suspect it was Stu, a real charmer, who'd corralled the usual pack of tourists that descended on Land's End every day. Maybe they took him for a tour guide, but he'd somehow persuaded them that, as a special bonus of their day out and absolutely free, they were about to be lucky enough to witness a truly historic event. So they'd better bloody well cheer. And they sure did!

All the support team were waiting for me, and some of our fantastic sponsors had made the journey too. That night, Angela and Sarah from Angel Call Handling in Andover cooked me, James and Stu a special celebratory meal in their Airbnb: my favourite Sunday roast with all the trimmings, even though it was a Tuesday. Roast beef and Yorkshire pudding had never tasted better. To this day, it's probably one of the best roasts I've ever eaten. It was a wonderful night in their happy company, but all the time at the back of my mind I was thinking about tomorrow, when I'd have to be back on that board, ploughing onwards. The Atlantic Ocean was coming my way, and autumn and winter would soon be here. The stark truth was that Phase One from the Thames Estuary to Land's End had, despite its undoubted challenges, been the easy bit. I'd reached the end of the beginning, nothing more. Now I'd have to face much stormier seas and winds that were blowing in straight from New York City. The days were getting shorter, the nights longer – those nights when I'd have to be out there paddling in the dark, all alone, cold, wet and just a bit miserable. In the days, weeks and months ahead of me, I was going to need Teddy Roosevelt's inspirational speech even more than when it had kept me going as I'd rowed across the Gate of Tears. Talking about the characteristics of the 'Man in the Arena', he'd said: 'If he fails, at least he fails while daring greatly, so that his place shall never be with those cold and timid souls who neither know victory nor defeat.'

Just one small problem, though: on the Great British Paddle, failure simply wasn't an option.

CHAPTER 12

SURFER'S PARADISE, PADDLEBOARDER'S HELL

I called him the David Hasselhoff of Cornwall. Handsome as hell and with a six-pack that wouldn't have looked out of place at a convention of Greek Gods, this dude knew everything there was to know about both surfing and prone paddling. Nobody could rival The Hoff's experience of the tides and winds of north Cornwall and how to overcome the serious challenges they posed. To add to the impression of overwhelming machismo, he was also a firefighter and senior RNLI lifeguard. His real name was Matt Thomas, and I wanted him to be my new best friend. I needed him. I really, really did. I was now facing obstacles I'd never even thought of, let alone planned for.

After navigating Land's End, the Great British Paddle had turned a corner, both literally and metaphorically. After my summer journey along the south coast of England, I now had to turn northwards into far more challenging seas – but I'd also turned a mental corner as a paddleboarder. No longer could anyone call me a novice. There was plenty I still had to learn, but few paddleboarders in the world had travelled as far as I had just done. I felt that I'd now justified the faith which my trainer Johnny Kivell, the team at the Water Skills Academy and the other expert boarders I'd met along the way had shown in me. All those lovely people who had never said out loud what they must have thought. At least now I could stand up straight among these folk. Just as well. Beyond the cliffs of Land's End, this was going to get really serious.

It was early September now, and the mornings were noticeably crisper, even though the daytime temperatures still carried the fading feel of late summer. The days were getting shorter, the autumnal equinox just a fortnight away. Along the way, the beaches were much less busy. The holiday families were packing up and heading home to their inland cities and towns. The cheering sight of the women in their bikinis was less frequent and the nudists were nowhere to be seen, having presumably felt the autumn nip on their todgers. The ice-cream and hot-dog vans were less numerous. With a long sigh, the British were gradually retreating indoors again, getting their thicker sweaters out of the drawer and wondering what was on the telly.

But there was no retreat for me. The morning after my arrival at Land's End, the celebratory roast beef hardly even digested, it was back to reality with a bump. With visibility less than 100 metres, I was barely able to see the coastline, and the swell was so strong I only managed a pathetic 7km the whole day. What was totally clear, however, was that the north coasts of Cornwall and Devon would be every bit as daunting as I'd expected. There were going to be some massively challenging paddles ahead.

The next day, I made it into the beautiful town of St Ives. Even on a day when the winds were fairly light, I could see at once why this stretch of Britain's coastline is known as a surfer's paradise and why thousands of elite surfers head there every year to ride the awesome swells. If I'd had any vague picture of myself doing the same on a paddleboard, I soon faced the truth. No way, José. No chance at all. All those surfing dudes were actively seeking the biggest possible waves while I was trying to avoid them. Paddleboarding is simply a different sport, a different process requiring another set of skills. It hadn't taken me long to pinpoint one of my major problems in this context: a phenomenon called 'clapotis'. This is when waves hit a strong barrier, such as a cliff face or a large rock, and then bounce off the barrier, consequently changing their direction in an unpredictable way. Really bad news for a paddleboarder. The clapotis issue meant having to go at least 5km out to sea in order to find calmer water. Tiring and time-consuming. Another one of nature's curveballs.

Yet again, cometh the hour, cometh the man – or woman. Luckily, I'd made online contact with Ginnie Betts, a Team GB athlete and top-class paddleboarder who had gone round Land's End herself. She boosted my ego by telling me how many paddlers far more experienced than me had been badly caught out on that iconic headland. Ginnie gave me loads of advice and insights about how to tackle these difficult northern coasts. And she gave me something else too: her partner Matt Thomas. Yep, him. The David Hasselhoff of Cornwall.

The first day I tried to set off out to sea from the beach at Perranporth was like a comedy film. I pushed myself out and the waves pushed me back, drenching me and scattering my kit. I tried again; they pushed me back again, as if saying, 'Piss off, Jord, we're for the big boys, not the likes of you.' This went on for two humiliating hours, much to the amusement of some of the surfers on the beach, who knew I was trying to do 'the impossible'. Bastards. But I got some much-needed encouragement from the women of the Bluetits Chill Swimmers club. These lovely ladies in their bathing caps, mostly middle-aged or older, took pity on me, cheering me on with each attempt I made to get out to sea and sighing in unison when I failed yet again. 'Come on, dear. Have another go. You'll make it next time; I know you will.'

'Aw, never mind, luv. If at first you don't succeed...'

But it was getting ridiculous. So, I sent an SOS to Ginnie Betts, and in no time over the horizon came The Hoff, back-lit by the sun, ripping off his shirt to show us his six-pack. Matt Thomas simply didn't recognise 'the impossible'. He went straight into sergeant-major mode and took no prisoners. Don't ask me how he managed to get me out to sea, but somehow with his help, his experience and the liberal use of unprintable expressions, I achieved the nearly bloody impossible, and by lying flat out on the board and paddling with my arms, I battled my way over the high ridges of foaming water out towards something calmer.

And perseverance pays. I didn't get too far that day, but there is always a silver lining in the Cornish clouds. Because on that same stressful day, I made it to the 1,000km mark of the Great British Paddle. Two fingers to those surfer dudes back on the beach and a big kiss to the Bluetits ladies.

It seemed silver linings came in pairs. That same day, a spectacular piece of good news broke through the autumn mists. My ship had come in. Captain Alex had just set sail from Southampton in the Great British Paddle's brand-new support boat. Having all had our fingers crossed for some time, the team had pulled off the coup of gaining sponsorship from the Royal Logistic Corps (RLC) of the British Army, who had generously agreed to provide the vessel in return for a bit of social media exposure for their excellent work. Hallelujah! I owe a big thank you to Neil Cuffley, a former RLC officer, who made this happen – what a legend!

It truly couldn't have come at a more important moment, just as the ride was about to get really rough. The long-lost *Coyote* had died on us only a few days into the expedition, and I'd gone for forty-six full days without it, depending entirely on James May and that hired van to follow me along the coastline. Despite his sterling efforts, it hadn't been the easiest or most efficient means of back-up. So, the news of a new boat was beyond brilliant. No more being squashed into the back of that cramped van with all the paddling gear plus James's film-making equipment, sometimes sleeping there if no onshore billet had turned up, sometimes eating powdered meals out of mess tins. James had quite loved all that, since it took him back to his days in the military; it took me back too, only I didn't want to go there. Maybe I was getting soft in my old age, but the thought of a proper cosy cabin was far more appealing. Captain Alex expected to reach us in about a week, in time to support me as I left the English coast, heading across to south Wales and then Ireland.

In the meantime, I made my way further along the coast

from Newquay to Padstow, then towards the mouth of the River Camel Estuary. There, the famous Doom Bar was waiting for me – not the well-known Cornish beer but the sandbar after which it is named. The Doom Bar is a natural phenomenon, composed mainly of marine sand continually carried up from the seabed. The mouth of the Camel Estuary, exposed to the Atlantic Ocean, is one of the most powerful in Europe; it is a highly dynamic nautical environment which makes the sandbar shift dramatically during heavy weather. Local sailors following me online had already sent advance warnings. There have been hundreds of shipwrecks and drownings on the Doom Bar, even quite recently, and it is famous as a place of ghosts and legends. One of these says that the sandbar was created by the Mermaid of Padstow out of revenge for being shot dead by a local man many moons ago. It was certainly a slightly spooky place to approach, bleak and unpredictable, and I consciously sharpened my senses to cope with whatever the Doom Bar might decide to throw at me. And somehow, I managed to avoid the worst fate of the Camel Estuary. That evening, we were billeted in Padstow with yet another lovely couple, Brian and Annie, who gave us a taste of Doom Bar beer accompanied by a warm shower and a home-cooked meal. Amber in colour and quite tart, it wasn't quite my pint, but I'd certainly rather have swallowed the beer than the waters of the sandbank as so many poor souls had done before me.

It was good news that I didn't get 'wrecked' on the Doom Bar that evening, because the next paddle was to throw me yet another curveball, much more scary than ghostly mermaids or the spirits of lost souls. In fact, it would be the most frightening event of the Great British Paddle so far.

Theoretically, it should have been a fairly easy ride. Captain Alex and the new boat were now close behind me, and we'd arranged to rendezvous in the port of Bude. But the boat had made faster progress than expected, and it tracked me down early. It was great to see Captain Alex in person again after a few weeks, but there had been a change of plan. I had been due to meet James May at 1 p.m. on a tiny beach below the ruins of Tintagel Castle, one of the very rare exit points on this jagged stretch of coastline. But now it had been arranged that the boat would sail on past me up to Ilfracombe because it was necessary to change the crew, and James had been told to drive up there in the van, so that all the kit and equipment could be loaded onto the boat. Once all that was done, the boat would return and pick me up by 5 or 6 p.m. To keep me going, they threw me down some snack food like I was a seal in the zoo. 'See you later!' called Captain Alex.

'Later' proved to be an infinitely flexible word. I paddled onwards, but by five or six no boat was yet visible. Nor by

7 p.m., by which time it was beginning to get dark, and there was no moonlight. I tried reaching the boat on my VHF radio, but there was no signal. What's more, the batteries were dying, and I kicked my own arse very hard for that fundamental schoolboy error. And now the swell was rising quickly. There was no chance of getting myself ashore, because the coastline was a solid wall of cliffs with no exit point. If I'd comforted myself that things couldn't get much worse, they suddenly did.

A big monster of a wave came out of the darkness and tore the paddle from my hands. In this sport, you might imagine that dropping the paddle would be a fairly regular occurrence, but actually it isn't. You might also ask why the paddle isn't attached to the paddler on a leash, just as the board itself is. The answer is that a leash is judged to be an impediment to the constant need to manoeuvre the paddle really quickly in response to the ever-changing fluctuations of the tide and the wind. If you drop the paddle in daylight, there's a decent chance of being able to retrieve it – but on a moonless night, it's a different story. This was a major incident. I'll make the obvious joke, just to get it out the way. Yep, I was up shit creek without a paddle.

Except this wasn't a joke. Not remotely. I wasn't even up a creek but, much more dangerously, out on the open sea somewhere between Tintagel Castle and Bude. Frightening doesn't even begin to describe it. I'd had some hairy experiences in the army, but this was worse. At least in a war zone you've usually got plenty of support if things get dangerous or go wrong. People looking out for you. This time, I was completely alone on the open sea.

I still presumed the boat was coming. And even though my VHF had died, Captain Alex should be able to pinpoint me via my Yellow Brick tracker. But exactly how close was the boat? 1 mile off? 5 miles? 10? I had no way of knowing. As I sat there on the board, I began to shiver a little, and not only from the cold. Now I knew something of what it must have felt like being in a *Titanic* lifeboat waiting for the *Carpathia* to arrive.

What worried me most was the risk of the board drifting helplessly into an unseen cliff face. So, I tried going down on my stomach, using my arms to move the board about a bit and maybe find the paddle still floating nearby. But it was a forlorn hope. I tried to block from my mind the worst possible outcome. The celebration at Land's End, the whoops and the cheers and the roast beef dinner had been less than a week ago, but it now felt like ancient history. All the positive-thinking techniques, all the inspirational quotes I'd memorised from Teddy Roosevelt and all the rest, began to wobble in my mind when faced with the reality of my situation. Maybe Teddy Roosevelt wouldn't have been so gung-ho if he'd ever found himself on a floating ironing board in the middle of the open sea in the pitch bloody dark. Maybe it would have been better after all if Johnny Kivell, instead of keeping schtum about his doubts, had come right out and said it. 'Listen, Jord, wake up and smell the coffee. This is just too much to take on.'

But he hadn't, and neither had any of the elite paddleboarders I'd come across. On the contrary, they'd all been totally supportive, behind me all the way. Remembering that now made me feel a bit ashamed. And even in the darkness, I could just make out the name I'd carefully painted on the board not long before. Caroline, who had so loved the water and who had shown so much bravery in the face of a terminal illness, not wanting to waste a second of the time she had left to her. A person I'd never known but whose courage somehow haunted me. So, I asked myself why I'd painted her name on the board if I wasn't going to respect her memory when push came to shove. Come on, Jordan, you're still on the board. Get a grip on yourself. You have survived much bigger challenges than this in Iraq, not to mention the pirates of Somalia. You've come through dengue fever and epilepsy, not to mention all the mental health stuff. You didn't get through all that to go tits up in sodding Devon.

And then, not long after, I saw a pinprick of light in the distance. At first, I didn't get my hopes up – and then I did. It was getting closer all the time. I used my own little flashlight in return. I began to hear voices shouting across the water, calling my name. It was Captain Alex and members of his crew. It was the new boat. They'd found me. 'Fancy meeting you here,' Alex called. 'Sorry, we got delayed. We had issues in the harbour waiting for people. It took for ever.'

Only when the boat came close did he realise the situation I'd been in and how serious it was. By now I was pretty distressed, and it showed on my face. And how glad I was to see somebody else on the deck, probably the person I needed more than anyone at that moment: Paula Reid. She and I went quietly down into the cabin and talked for a little while, then she left me alone for an hour or so. There was little point in blaming anyone or yelling at people; regardless of how much I might have wanted to, it had to be remembered that they were all volunteers, doing this for a good cause out of the kindness of their hearts. These things happen. But it had been a big screw-up and potentially lethal.

Afterwards, the team discussed what lessons were to be taken from this incident. Apart from the obvious one – to avoid dropping the bloody paddle – the other lessons were to carry a spare paddle and spare batteries for the comms devices. But maybe the biggest lesson was not to embark on an expedition like this at night without having a support boat close at all times. For the past fifty days plus, with James May's help and despite the summer storms and the gammy leg, I'd somehow got away with it. But getting unlucky tonight only emphasised how really lucky I had been up till now.

After we'd lost use of the *Coyote*, the sensible thing might have been to suspend the expedition till another affordable vessel could be sourced. But that would have risked puncturing so much of the excitement that had built up not just within the team but, more importantly, among the sponsors and all the supporters and donors, which had been steadily growing day by day. So, James May and I had never hesitated for an instant. We'd both been soldiers, after all; when Plan A fails, you just go to Plan B, even if it's not ideal. And that's what we'd done. And, as I've written, Plan B had brought with it one of the most rewarding aspects of the Great British Paddle: without the support boat, our daily need for bed and board had allowed us to meet so many great and generous people. People who had not just given us food and shelter but also encouragement. So, all in all, no regrets. Not even that night, as I sat warming myself up and calming myself down inside the beautiful new boat, a 40ft Elan yacht named the *Spirit of St George II*. I don't know why the boat had been christened such, but it seemed an appropriate name for this expedition. That night was a chastening experience, and I wasn't remotely ashamed of having been shit scared. I'd learnt in the military that only fools aren't scared and that brave men always are. Yet I told myself there must be no more wobbles, either physical or mental. I'd try to channel a bit of St George's spirit. There would be plenty more dragons coming my way.

CHAPTER 13

THE IRISH JIG

Two steps forward, one step back. One step forward, two steps back. This was the nature of the crazy jig I was about to dance with the perilous Irish Sea.

The Night of the Lost Paddle, as I came to think of it, was in some senses the real end of the first phase of the expedition, rather than that memorable moment of reaching Land's End. The arrival of the new support boat marked the end of the first fifty or so days, when I'd been more vulnerable than I cared to admit. And now, the cast of characters in this story changes a little.

One of the unfortunate aspects of the drama at Tintagel Castle was losing the chance to say a proper goodbye to James May, who had to leave the team as soon as he'd dropped off the kit and equipment at Bude. He'd given me nearly two months of his life without a penny in return, but like all of us he had bills to pay and needed to start earning money again.

His contribution to the Great British Paddle had been invaluable. His beautiful videos and his diary of my daily progress had been the most important tool in firing public interest and keeping it burning throughout the expedition, even in the fallow days caused by poor weather. But his contribution went way beyond that. He'd been my companion and my support every kilometre of the way. Without James, the past fifty days would have been impossible. Not that we hadn't had the odd moments of mutual irritation, usually when the terrain or the road network made it difficult for him to track me down. All those 'Where the hell are you?' moments. Or when he'd greeted me on a beach at the end of a sweltering paddle and gave me the can of Coke I'd been fantasising about for at least three hours. 'Bloody hell, James,' I'd said. 'This Coke is *warm*.'

'Oh, sorry, Jord, so you wanted a *cold* Coke?'

'Of course I bloody did. I've been on that effing board in the sun all day long. Is that too much to ask?'

'Well, you should have *said* you wanted a cold one,' he replied with a straight face. 'Christ, Jordan. You're *so* high maintenance you army blokes.'

For all those weeks we'd been joined at the hip, and I was really going to miss his banter and his camaraderie. The compensation was feeling sure we'd now be friends for ever.

But the arrival of the *Spirit of St George II* was a massive blessing. Now, I was about to do the longest stretch of paddling of the expedition so far: the crossing from Lundy Island off the north coast of Devon across the wide Bristol Channel to the coast of south Wales. A journey during which I was going to be infinitely further from dry land than I'd been before. One which would leave me totally exposed to fierce westerly winds roaring in off the Atlantic Ocean. A passage which, without the boat, would have been potentially suicidal.

The operating base for the crossing was to be the beautiful Lundy Island, surely one of the most scenically stunning places in Britain. On the day we sailed towards it from the Devon coast, it was wreathed in a fog that only parted when we got quite close and the island suddenly rose up from the sea in walls of towering cliff. It was breathtaking, mystical, even a little eerie. At first, we saw no sign at all of human habitation, only the seabirds swooping and diving all around us. Those cliffs and the island's position on major migration routes make it a haven for many species of birdlife. Now owned by the National Trust and with only a tiny human population mostly working in wildlife conservation, Lundy feels totally isolated from the modern world. At night, when the daytime visitors have returned to their Devon resorts, the stars shine like tiny diamonds in its clear, unpolluted sky. It is a spiritual place; a place where you can reconnect with yourself. How nice it would have been to rest here for a while. But there was no chance of that, because now I had to pull the big one out of the bag.

Maybe the gods were trying to apologise to me after The Night of the Lost Paddle, because they gave me the most beautiful day. The sky was blue, the sea not too rough. The new support boat was close by, and Captain Alex was playing classics from the '80s and '90s. We also had a welcome new crew mate in Kate Doison, a volunteer from the RNLI and the founder of Coast to Coast Water Safety. Kate had a dream of being the first woman to prone paddle from the mainland to Lundy Island, so we were very proud to help her fulfil that goal; she was a true water woman too and gave me lots of great advice. Above all, we had the magical companionship of the dolphins in greater numbers than ever before. Pod after pod appeared in the water, doing their travel guide thing to escort me over to Wales. Instead of being the tough experience I'd expected, the crossing turned out to be one of my favourite paddles of the whole expedition. Paula Reid took some photos for her mother, who is a painter and who created a beautiful seascape picture which I'll always treasure. That day was also my personal best so far, notching up nearly 65km between Lundy and Milford Haven in south Wales. The old blue therapy really was working that day. If I'd ever, however briefly, doubted its power, that one day brought it all back to me.

Back in Devon, I'd met up with a terrific woman called Cal Major. Cal had been the first person to paddleboard from Land's End to John O'Groats on the northern tip of Scotland, so she was the ideal person to give me advice about the next leg of my trip. But she gave me a lot more than just that. Cal is a passionate advocate of the benefits that spending time on the water have on mental health, having suffered, just like me, from periods of anxiety and depression. 'The water is the place where I heal from grief or loss,' she said. 'But it's also where I feel most empowered and hopeful.'

'I totally understand that. It's the same for me too,' I replied. I told Cal about having stopped my medication, and I found myself getting a bit emotional as I did so.

'Well, the meds are certainly needed at times,' she said. 'No use denying it. But I agree. The ocean is the best medication. For you and me anyway, Jordan. For other people, it might be the mountains or the lake or the local park. It doesn't matter what it is. It's making the connection with nature that matters. Everyone has some place that really sparks something inside them.'

'It's definitely the water that does it for me,' I said.

'Me too,' said Cal. 'Whenever I've been low, the worst days

have always been when I couldn't get onto the ocean. It's where I feel most alive.'

On that fantastic day crossing to Wales in the September sunshine, I just knew she was right. I could literally feel it working on my body and mind. At long last, after these lengthy, painful weeks, my injured leg seemed finally to be on the mend, and I was ever more convinced that I no longer needed the pills messing with my brain. All my brain needed, all my soul needed, was this connection with nature about which Cal Major was so passionate and inspirational. Once again, I felt so lucky, privileged even, that I was where I was and doing what I was doing. Every human being should be able to say that, but so often in our lives it isn't true. So, whenever, by design or just by good fortune, such times come our way, we must recognise them, treasure them and store them away to help us face the tougher stuff. In my case, that tougher stuff was just about to happen. Its name was Ireland.

• • •

I'd had this nice picture in my mind of my mum and dad, my aunties and uncles and my old mates from school all coming down to Blackpool Beach to meet me. It would've been such a tonic to see them. Nice too to see that bloody great tower, the endless prom and the famous illuminations. All those familiar landmarks of my youth. I could hear my mum fussing about what I was wearing and urging me to wrap up well etc. Thankfully, some things never change.

But it wasn't to be. The option of paddling up the west coast of England would expose me to the weather much more than crossing the Irish Sea and going up the east coast of Ireland, using its land mass to shelter me from the worst of the Atlantic weather systems. That had been the view of so many of the elite paddleboarders who had been kind enough to offer advice, and it was certainly the view of Captain Alex. So, that was that. Crossing the Irish Sea was the plan.

This was the moment when a new cast of characters joined the Great British Paddle. Captain Alex had only come to deliver the boat and was now heading home again, so three complete strangers were now to be my 'family'. The skipper was now Darren Cox, known as Daz. He was still a serving member of the British Army and the Army Sailing Association, and his designated job was to look after the boat, which is often hired out for adventure training work or just private charters. Daz is a fine yachtsman and a great guy, though he possesses a lot of that black humour that serving military personnel often have. I was used to it, of course, but sometimes civilians could find his chaffing and insults a bit hard to take. Not everybody likes being called a fucking tosser with bollocks the size of garden peas. But he has a heart of gold, and the expedition was hugely lucky to have him.

Tori Wells was a farm girl from south Wales who was an adult volunteer in the Army Cadet Force. She had attended one of the talks I regularly give to the cadets and had followed my adventures online ever since. Like me, she is passionate about the outdoors, and she had become a qualified climbing instructor. Tori had felt very affected by the complicated issues impacting young people around the world, especially during this grim year of Covid, and grasped this chance to do her bit to help at least a handful of kids in Africa. Most vitally for an expedition like this one, Tori had just the right attitude, willing to turn her hand to anything, with a strong enough personality to deal with Daz's brand of humour.

Alfie Marsh was a young lad from Edinburgh who was to replace James May as our film-maker and photographer. Though only nineteen, Alfie was steadily building a career posting videos online and had already toured with some bands in Asia and supported adventurers like me in tough environments around the world. But he was now looking for a really big adventure project that would let him do more challenging and experimental work and really put him on the map. When we accepted him, he had only fifteen hours to get from Edinburgh down to south Wales. On the way, he texted to say his car had crashed somewhere in the north of England. Yeah, right, we all thought. Another bloody teenager who's changed his mind and is messing us about. But we'd hugely misjudged him; the car-crash story was true. Alfie's parents dashed down to pick him up from the accident site and delivered him to us in south Wales just in time. Like Tori Wells, he was willing to turn his hand to anything and soon learnt how to crew a boat. Alfie often wore Crocs and was soon named 'Croco' by everyone. He was a lovely lad with a big heart: a great addition to the team. Someone who was, like Tori, quite simply 'right'.

I'd not had much to do with the recruitment of this new team, as project manager Captain Alex had fixed all that, putting out advertisements online. Amazingly, over 100 people had applied to join the Great British Paddle. It was striking how many had military backgrounds – people who were used to physical stress and strain, used to pushing their boundaries and getting out of their comfort zones. That was what they thrived on; it was part of who they were. But Alex had chosen very carefully, because it wasn't always about getting the best people in terms of particular skills or experience of extreme adventuring. In fact, we'd politely turned down some candidates who possessed these qualifications because somehow they just didn't feel right. What we wanted was people who would be committed and loyal and give 110 per cent. Life on the boat would be claustrophobic, the conditions challenging and maybe even dangerous, and there would be no pay. What wasn't to like?

This new team proved themselves before we'd even left the mooring at Milford Haven. It was soon going to be my birthday, but who knew where I would be on the actual day, so they threw me a surprise party in advance. The real and wonderful surprise was the arrival of my dad from Blackpool and my daughter Evie from Andover. And James May pitched up too, bringing his lovely family with him. The team had kept it as secret as *This Is Your Life*. Tori cooked up a fine dinner for all these people, and we had a great evening on board. It had been almost two months since I'd last seen my daughter, though it felt even longer, and Evie had brought me little cakes with 'GBP' iced on them.

Though my dad enjoyed regaling everyone with stories of what a pain in the rear end I'd been as a lad, I knew he was proud of what I was doing. David Wylie has always been my inspiration. Like me, he was a boy from a humble background who had been 'made' by his time in the military. That was where he'd gained his values in life – the same values he'd tried so hard to pass on to me, even during the teenage years when I wasn't listening. It was only when I entered the army myself and absorbed the same ethos and codes of conduct that had formed my father that they finally sank in. In those later years, when for a while I'd lost sight of all that and been dazzled by money, posh Mayfair hotels and racehorses, it must have hurt my dad to witness the transformation. But I hoped and believed that he approved of the new direction I'd found in my life. Nothing ever made me prouder than when he and I marched, with our boots polished and medals shining, through Blackpool every year on Remembrance Sunday. However far apart our lives took us, that was when we always came together again. Man and boy. Father and son. Chip off the old block.

And I knew Evie approved of me too. Sometimes children don't like it when their parents do 'weird' stuff. They want their parents to be just like everyone else's and certainly not to be embarrassing. But my Evie didn't seem to be afflicted with that. In her case, her school chums were probably sick to death of hearing about how many kilometres I'd chalked up on any given day.

That special evening on the new boat was wonderful, but looking back on it I realise that it unintentionally made things a bit tougher. After just one day of being together, saying goodbye again to Dad and Evie was really hard. I felt homesick and emotional, though I tried not to show it. I didn't know when I'd see either of them again, or what challenging times I might face before that happened. Almost certainly, I'd be missing Remembrance Day this year; Dad would have to spend the day alone. Despite the cheery presence of the new boat crew and the fun of getting to know them, I felt a wave of sadness sweep over me when my father and my daughter drove away from the harbour at Milford Haven. There's nothing like the bond with your own flesh and blood. It's visceral and powerful. The heartbeat of everything.

•   •   •

The Irish Sea didn't seem to want me. The plans of the Great British Paddle didn't seem to fit in with its own schedule. And that schedule was to throw a major strop and do everything it could to stop me reaching the Emerald Isle. Having just paddle-vaulted the Bristol Channel in perfect weather with no trouble at all, and even though it was a much longer trip of about 90km, I'd felt fairly confident about the crossing to Ireland. Wrong.

The weather now began to break down, though the deterioration was gradual at first. Yet again, that discrepancy arose between Captain Alex's forecasts and the reality on the spot. On a perfectly decent day, we embarked from Milford Haven for the big crossing. Without any major problems thus far, I was about a third of the way across the Irish Sea when

Alex texted Daz to warn us that a big storm would hit within twelve hours, and to stay safe I must get off the paddleboard and the boat should race as fast as possible the rest of the way to the shelter of the nearest Irish harbour, because that would be quicker than returning to Wales.

Daz and I were extremely reluctant to chuck in the paddle as the going had been good so far. Friction arose, and a few muttered expletives too, but Captain Alex was the project manager and that had to be respected. It was in our DNA to obey the orders of a superior officer. But, oh boy, in retrospect how we wished we'd disobeyed, gone AWOL and risked the court martial. But we didn't. Instead, I got off the board and the boat sailed as fast as it could into the shelter of the Irish coast to ride out the coming storm. But the storm never came. With hindsight, I could easily have finished the paddle to Ireland and saved us all a week's wasted time. But that's the way the potato cake crumbles.

We were now in an Irish harbour called Kilmore Quay, near the ferry port of Rosslare. This was swiftly rechristened Killjoy Quay because it was a pretty miserable bolthole. Partly because it was semi-industrial, partly because almost everything there was now shut due to Covid restrictions. After the breathing space of the summer months, the situation in Britain and Ireland was getting worse again, and many yachting facilities on the Irish coast were beginning to close down. This was a major worry for us, as the support boat would have an ongoing need for fuel, food and water supplies, as well as access to showers and a laundry. It was also clear that we would have to budget for more mooring fees than we'd bargained for as we progressed up the east coast of Ireland.

The next morning, the storm still nowhere to be seen, we sailed back out from Ireland to the point in the Irish Sea where I'd abandoned the paddle yesterday. And guess what? Just as we got there, just as the board was going into the water, a massive bank of black cloud appeared. Storm Aiden, a good old Irish name, had finally arrived. A return to Ireland was impossible, so in order to escape its clutches we had to sail back, as fast as we could, to the safety of Wales. Even more expletives filled the air above the boat. Sadly, all this led to yet more friction between Daz and Captain Alex, and there was – rarely for this expedition – what you might call 'negative energy' around. Or, in common parlance, they had a bit of a barney.

Storm Aiden powered into Wales and south-west Britain like an unleashed beast, bringing Arctic temperatures with it. You could forget about autumn, 'season of mists and mellow fruitfulness' and all that crap. This felt like going straight into winter. Right now, the Great British Paddle wasn't having the luck of the Irish one little bit. But nobody else was either. The

Met Office announced that, during 2020, the Atlantic Ocean had served up a total of twenty-four tropical or sub-tropical cyclones, twenty-three named storms, two major hurricanes and eight small ones. It also cheerily told us that at least five more named storms would be coming our way during autumn and winter. No wonder people emigrate.

Even once Storm Aiden had done its worst and moved on, the weather remained unpredictable. And so, my jig with the Irish Sea resumed. Over the next week or so, I'd take a few steps back out into the sea, then it would push me back towards Milford Haven. The next day, if there was a window, I'd make another small thrust westwards, only to be shoved back again to the shelter of Wales. Back and forth we danced across the steel-grey sea. It was tedious, frustrating and enervating. A long day in rough conditions, and at the end of it maybe only a few kilometres of actual paddling achieved.

Once, after a rare window of eight hours, I managed to cover 50km, which got me to over halfway across the Irish Sea, before we had to race back to Wales yet again. About the most exciting thing that happened was the day when Daz, at the wheel, shouted to us all to come quickly. 'Look! There!' he yelled. 'Shark!'

And sure enough, there it was, the grey fin cutting through the water like a knife through butter. The first and only shark sighting of the entire Great British Paddle. It was a beautiful and awe-inspiring moment, though I was suddenly quite glad not to be on the paddleboard that morning. I pictured those vast jaws rearing up from the sea, hunting for their breakfast: first the paddle, then the board, then me. I found myself channelling Richard Dreyfuss and Roy Scheider. 'Close the beaches! Close the beaches!'

Not that there was anyone on the beaches, not in this shocking weather. However pretty it was and however brilliant the folk we met, I began to be weary of the sight of Milford Haven. Was this the endgame? Was this as far as the Great British Paddle was ever going to go?

Worse yet, I started getting sick in another way too. To my surprise, I discovered that I am prone to seasickness, and I started chucking up over the side with monotonous regularity. Till then, I'd never thought of myself as a bad sailor. During my years in maritime security around the Horn of Africa, I'd usually been totally fine; the sub-tropical conditions there meant fairly placid seas. Only during a couple of storms had I been really ill, and I'd put that down to the unusual ferocity of those events. But then, in the middle of the Irish Sea, I realised that I did indeed suffer from this most hellish of ailments. The only good news was that my nausea was confined to being on the boat; I was usually fine when I was paddling – maybe something to do with the closer proximity to the water. Apart from the misery of feeling sick, there was the added drawback of losing the energy I needed from my food, so I became dehydrated and tired more quickly at the very time I needed energy most. It's so strange how seasickness affects some people and not others, presumably due to the fine mechanisms of the inner ear. It certainly pissed me off that while I, green at the gills, was trying to hold down another load of projectile vomit, Daz, Tori and Alfie were happily wolfing down curry or spag bol, the smells of which were enough in themselves to send me rushing for the side of the boat.

With so little progress being made, I occupied most of my time online, asking our already generous donors if they could possibly help us out even more to pay for the large amounts of fuel now being consumed by so many abortive trips. As always, they came up trumps, something which was always humbling. By now it was Day 59 of the Great British Paddle, late September, two months since I'd left the Essex Marina as a wobbly and nervous novice. To amuse myself, I made a list of statistics for our online followers about the expedition so far:

- 1,300km paddled.
- Thirty-nine dolphins spotted.
- Hundreds of seals.
- Three trips to A&E with my infected leg.
- Eight paddles through the night.

- Over 400,000 calories consumed.
- Three jellyfish stings.
- Fifty-one days with no support boat.
- Longest paddle of sixteen hours and twenty-three minutes.
- Personal best of 65km in one day.
- Nearly £15,000 raised so far for the school in Djibouti.

Over the past two months, my board had taken quite a beating, so this lay-off was an ideal chance for *Caroline* to be given a makeover by Gareth of Dale Sailing in Milford Marina. Gareth was a serious rower, soon to cross the Atlantic in the Talisker Challenge, the world's most prestigious rowing marathon, in which competitors row from the Canary Islands to Antigua over 3,000 miles of ocean – something which made my day trip across the Gate of Tears seem a bit of a doddle. On this expedition, I was constantly amazed by the folk I bumped into in the sailing and water sports communities. So-called ordinary people who did the most extraordinary things. Rowing over oceans, sailing round the globe, breaking records. If I'd ever been deluded enough to imagine that what I was doing somehow made me extra special, the delusion didn't last long. I was just one of an amazing gang of worldwide adventurers and honoured to be among them.

But by now, the struggle to paddle across the Irish Sea once and for all was getting us down. Apart from the test of physical endurance, it was a mental challenge too. But, hallelujah, after almost a week of being locked in that absurd and infuriating dance with the sea, I finally made it across to the Irish coast at Arklow in County Wicklow. I'd now paddled to three countries – England, Wales and Ireland – and I'd soon be heading towards Northern Ireland to make that a fourth. And that day, as the Irish coast grew closer, yet another pod of magnificent dolphins came out to meet me, immediately followed by a beautiful rainbow. I decided this must be the Irish tourist board giving me a belated welcome and apologising for the nightmare of the past week. Better late than never.

It was certainly nicer to watch the dolphins going past the board than another long dark object I'd recently encountered in the water. At first, I thought it was just another piece of flotsam, a splinter of driftwood. Then I realised it was something quite different. An absolute stonker of a turd – and it was coming towards me at a rate of knots. Ugh. I was paddling quite close to the boat at that moment and saw Tori suddenly appear on deck. 'Hey, Tori, have you just had a No. 2?' I called over.

'How do you know that?' she shouted back, smiling.

'Cos it's swum out to meet me,' I said. 'It's like a bloody torpedo trying to push me off the board.'

Not a conversation I'd normally have with a young lady, but Tori was not the sort to be easily embarrassed, so we had a great laugh. Such silly episodes were of real value in keeping us all cheerful during those difficult days. We were confined together in a small space, and we were all aware of the need to minimise the little ordinary tensions that such proximity inevitably brought. And by now, there wasn't much we didn't know about one another. Warts and all. Anyway, since poor Tori had had to watch me throwing up often enough, her retaliatory assault with a large floater seemed fair enough.

But things seemed to have become even more bleak in Ireland since our brief glimpse of it a week earlier at Kilmore Quay. Now, we learnt that our next three scheduled harbour and marina stops were closed until further notice. Some big decisions would soon have to be made. If the *Spirit of St George II* was unable to move on, maybe I'd have to go solo again, with just a sleeping bag and a tent. A grim prospect. Bloody hell, I'd only had the home comforts of the new boat for about a fortnight; now things would be even worse than the glorious days of James's hired van.

The good news was that the Irish media had woken up to the Great British Paddle, and I was doing plenty of interviews. I now heard myself pledge that if we could hit a total of £20,000 in donations by 31 October, I'd do a paddle for twenty-four hours dressed as a witch, with the paddle as my obvious broomstick. I'd look like a complete idiot of course, but who cares? Bubble, bubble, toil and a lot of trouble, but

I was shameless in doing anything I could to keep the funds coming in.

I managed one mighty paddle of 38km up the coast to Wicklow before the next bloody storm was due to hit. This time, in order to take shelter Daz had taken the boat ahead of me up to the Malahide Marina near Dublin. But then the thorny question of how much longer we might be able to use the support boat was suddenly taken out of our hands. Daz, a member of the British Army, was now suddenly required to skipper other boats elsewhere, and he had to leave us after only three weeks. A big blow. Captain Alex urgently searched for a new skipper, but until one was found the *Spirit of St George II* would be out of commission and imprisoned in the marina. Bloody hell. It had been nice while it lasted – but at least we still had it as accommodation. Yet, if I wanted to make any progress, every day I'd have to be driven from Malahide Marina back to the latest starting point, then drive all the way back again after the paddle. For that, we'd need a support driver with a van, but such a way of doing things was going to be a major pain in the arse – unless of course I used a tent, which as autumn got a tighter grip wasn't exactly appealing. The Covid regulations were constantly changing and making our lives very difficult, and sitting around endlessly while we waited for a new skipper was a dreadful waste of time. Every day, winter was getting closer.

The seas I was now facing every day seemed a lifetime away from the sunny south of England in July and early August. I would look back and smile to myself about those days I'd thought were the hardest ever, going round Dungeness, Portland Bill and The Lizard. These now seemed a piece of cake. The sea now was far more unforgiving, the water far colder, the wind biting into my face much more sharply. Though the Malahide Marina was technically closed, they very generously agreed, because we were a good cause, to let us moor there for three weeks for free, while Captain Alex tried to find a new skipper. But now there was the additional problem that any new skipper entering Ireland might have to quarantine for fourteen days. So, for now it was just Tori, Alfie and me. They were both brilliant and willing, even though they weren't trained to the highest levels in things like map-reading, and we really needed that skill in order to continue. The problems facing the Great British Paddle seemed to be mounting steadily.

As always, there were a few knights in shining armour. A generous local company supplied us with a free van and insurance. A kind landowner allowed us the use of her small private beach as a launch point. But though some small progress was usually achieved, it was a slow and frustrating business leaving at dawn and driving to and from Malahide every day, even though the standard of our carpool karaoke was pretty impressive. And the prospect of one of Tori's beef and vegetable stews at the end of each day helped to keep me going.

During this frustrating period, it was fortunate that we all got along pretty well. Tori and I both had our own tiny cabins, and Alfie and his girlfriend Mia, who had joined us for a while, slept in the main cabin. The space was small, and Alfie's film-making equipment spread all over the shop made the main space look a bit like a student flat. There was little privacy, but the inevitable small tensions which arose were always handled with maturity, everyone making allowances for the situation and always remembering the reason why we were there.

All the time too, the information on Covid seemed to be changing and was tricky to pin down. It began to be difficult to know when and where we could stock up on food supplies for the boat and fuel for the van. It was always important to me to do the right thing during this expedition so that no negative image could ever dent its reputation. Therefore, every rule and regulation had to be followed, no matter how irksome. The school in Djibouti had to be built without the slightest taint about how the money for it had been raised. But yet again, I began to wonder if the Great British Paddle might have to be abandoned, defeated not by storms or an infected leg but by this scary crisis that was sweeping the entire world.

It was now Day 76 of the Great British Paddle; I'd covered nearly 1,500km and I reckoned I deserved a day off. So, I took it. But I had no intention of sitting on my arse watching videos and eating crisps. I was going to do something possibly even crazier than my current day job on the ironing board – because I'd been thrown a challenge no extreme adventurer would be able to resist.

CHAPTER 14

BUSMAN'S HOLIDAY

Leaving Tori and Alfie in charge of the boat, I jumped on a plane from Dublin to Manchester. My girlfriend Megan, thoughtful and supportive as ever, picked me up and drove me across into Yorkshire to a little place called Boulby, somewhere I'd never heard of. This was to be the site of one of the oddest adventures anybody anywhere had yet dreamed up.

It was called 'Beneath the Surface', an event organised for Mental Health Day by the Army Cadet Force as part of its 'Healthy Minds' programme. The objective was simple: to draw attention to the fact that it's often not possible to know what might be going on inside someone else's mind, and the need to always be aware of that. To dramatise this issue, a marathon was to be run literally beneath the surface – 1,000 metres under the sea down a working mine. Brilliant idea.

There would be relatively few runners taking part, but at

the same time over 1,500 young people in the Army Cadet Force would be completing an online training session about the vital importance of mental health. Both the marathon itself and the online event would be contenders for inclusion in the *Guinness Book of World Records*. Since all this was obviously very close to my heart, since I was an ambassador for the Army Cadets and since it could help me raise more money for the school, I was keen to give it my best shot – but it was certainly a busman's holiday.

If there is a greater contrast between the open sea and an underground mine, I can't imagine what it might be. I'd not be chilled to the bone but sweltering instead. I'd not be soaking wet but bone-dry except for my own sweat. No longer on the surface of the water, I'd be 1,000 metres under the floor of the North Sea.

The Boulby mine isn't used for the usual excavation of coal but for polyhalite, a mineral widely used in fertilisers, and the route of the marathon would be around its labyrinthine network of tunnels. 'At least I'll be nice and warm for once,' I said to the safety officer as we went down in the lift.

'You don't know how right you are, Jord,' he replied, in that way people have when they're telling you something which they know and you don't.

Sure enough, it was one hell of a culture shock. So used

to being cold, my body was now faced with extreme heat – about 40 degrees at least – and my lungs, used to unpolluted sea air, now encountered a dry, dusty atmosphere. But the essential issue was that for nearly three months I'd been standing or kneeling on a tiny paddleboard. During that time, I'd done no fitness training at all. I'd hardly even gone for a walk when on dry land. By contrast, most of the other runners, mostly miners, were used to this environment, had been training for months and were raring to go.

It wasn't an easy route by any means. The tunnels weren't level but went up hill and down dale, corkscrewing around corners. It wasn't long before I began to get dreadful cramps in both legs. Soon it was physical hell, possibly the most pain I'd ever experienced in my life. One of the other runners did his best to help me along, as did one of the miners, who was a rescue medic, but I was nearly screaming in agony. A knot of muscle as big as a golf ball kept popping up below the skin of my thigh. If I tried to massage it and push it down, it would then pop up in another location. It was like something out of *Alien*. 'You want to give up, mate. You're never going to make it,' said one of the miners. He said it more than once as he went past me. 'Pack it in, mate. Do yourself a favour.' I began to wonder if his own ego and desire to win was involved and if he was just trying to knock a competitor out of the marathon. But this guy didn't know me, and his words only had the opposite effect. Fuck you, I thought. I'm going to finish this. Part of the reason behind the event was to emphasise to young Army Cadets the need for mental discipline as an aid to general mental health, so I bloody well wasn't going to be intimidated into defeat. Focus on the goal, not on the pain of achieving it.

It was also necessary for at least two people to complete the marathon for the event to stand a chance of getting into Guinness, so, as somebody had already dropped out with breathing problems, I didn't want to be another reason for failure. Thankfully, five runners managed to complete it, including me. But I was in a pretty rough old state at the finish.

Still, it was well worth it. Beneath the Surface broke two world records that day: one for the deepest ever underground marathon and one for the highest number of people ever to take part simultaneously in a mental health online training course. But the real objective had been far more important: remembering that you can never truly know what other people might be going through when there are no visible signs or symptoms of distress. Nobody understood that better than me; however, those who really need to grasp that truth are those who don't suffer from severe mental health problems themselves but who come into contact with those who do. And that could be anyone. A partner, a parent, a child. The friend you have a pint with on a Friday night whose marriage you know to be rocky but who seems to be coping. The neighbour who's lost her job due to the pandemic and is struggling to feed her kids but who still smiles and says good morning. The boss who seems to be even more of an awkward bastard lately. So, before you speak, judge or make a negative comment online, just stop and think about how damaging your words could be to somebody else's spirit. If you can't be kind to others, then at least you can be quiet. And never forget it could be you next. However strong and resilient we think we are, life can sometimes turn on us and, like the black dog, bare its teeth. Take it from me.

'You're nuts, you know that, don't you?' said the lovely adjudicator from Guinness World Records as I rested my shell-shocked legs before heading straight to Manchester Airport and back to the paddleboard…

• • •

In the nick of time, another of our knights in shining armour appeared. One who knew how to skipper a boat. His name was Max Rivers, a young guy who had been teaching sailing in Greece but was now flying back to the UK and would have to sit out fourteen days in quarantine before he could get over to Ireland. Even though we had to wait, it was great to know he was coming.

In the meantime, bit by bit, I inched my way up the east coast of Ireland, at long last getting past Dublin and the Malahide Marina, where the boat was still moored. There had even been a few decent weather windows. One day I even managed 34km, the longest single paddle for weeks – and then I topped that with a run of 44km. Now and again, Alfie would jump on the spare inflatable paddleboard and join me for a while. It was always good to have his company, especially in the lonely darkness of an early morning. But by Christ, it was getting so much colder. One time, I had to break the ice off the leash connecting me to the board. It was an omen.

And then, back from sunny Greece and like a god descending from Mount Olympus to bless us mere mortals, Max Rivers arrived. He was in his early twenties but was wise beyond his years and had just finished a degree in outdoor education and adventure. I knew instantly that he was going to be a brilliantly capable skipper. At once, he took control of the *Spirit of St George II* and evaluated the boat and all of us too, working out our strengths and weaknesses. Despite his relative youth, he exuded confidence and experience, reminding me of many of the young officers I'd known in the military. He had a good sense of humour and excellent people skills. He could even cook better than any of us. If I'd been that way inclined, I might even have fallen in love. After our recent difficult weeks, his presence was like a shot in the arm. It was also a relief; once again, I felt the expedition was in safe hands.

On Day 88 of the Great British Paddle, having chalked up over 1,600km, I crossed over into the waters of Northern Ireland, the fourth country on my journey. The usual gang of dolphins and seals escorted me over the border. By now, I almost believed that they knew when I was coming or when I deserved a bit of moral support.

On Day 90, I did another interview with Kay Burley of Sky News. As always, Kay was being a total legend in keeping up public awareness of the expedition and helping the donations come in. As yet, I still didn't know the spectacular contribution this lady would ultimately make to the Great British Paddle. If somebody had told me then what that contribution would be, I'd never have believed them.

Almost wherever we went, the knights in shining armour were never far away. My beloved Army Cadet family had a strong presence in every part of the UK, and now a dynamic woman called Alison Campbell from one of their Northern Ireland battalions organised a huge donation of provisions from a whole gang of local people and businesses – butchers and bakers, grocers and fishmongers. Such generosity and such a help to our budget. Every pound we didn't have to spend on the expedition's running costs meant another pound heading out to Djibouti. Another brick in the wall.

It was also encouraging to know that I wasn't the only nutter out on the water in early November. One day I saw this guy swimming not far from me. Since we were the only two folk in the vicinity, it seemed rude not to stop for a natter. Incredibly, this turned out to be the remarkable Henry O'Donnell, who was attempting to be the first person to finswim around Ireland – or indeed around any country in the world. Like paddleboarding, finswimming is one of those fringe water sports of which the great mass of people still haven't heard. Basically, you propel yourself through the water by means of one or two small metal fins. You can do it either on the surface or beneath it with a snorkel or sub-aqua equipment. Henry was a 56-year-old grandfather and ex-military, a veteran of the Special Forces and an Irish Army Ranger. He was tough as old boots, with a long history of extreme adventures behind him. I was awed by what he was trying to do. I reckoned that paddling on the surface of these late autumn waters was challenge enough; the idea of being totally immersed in them seemed almost super-human.

Like me, Henry was putting himself through it for excellent causes: the Irish Cancer Society and Water Safety Ireland. I've met plenty of inspirational people in my life, but

Henry O'Donnell truly stood out. Twenty years older than me, he was still pushing his boundaries, still seeking new ways to challenge himself. If I'm doing a quarter of what he does when I reach his age, I'll be pretty pleased with myself. We live in such an ageist society, where it's assumed that getting older is a curse and somehow a lessening of ourselves. Henry was one of those folk who showed that it can mean the very opposite.

Under Max Rivers's excellent captaincy, I continued to creep up the coast of Northern Ireland, though increasingly it was that familiar one day on, one day off scenario as the weather continued to be volatile. Then, on Halloween an eight-hour window allowed me to do nearly 50km, which was bloody fantastic. Even more fantastic when you think I was dressed up as a witch, as I'd promised my online followers I would be. I don't think I scared anybody, though, except myself when I looked in a mirror.

And then it came. The 100th day. When I embarked on the Great British Paddle, I imagined that the total circumnavigation of Great Britain might be completed in that time. Talk about naïve. Talk about crazy. But I was still standing. I was still in the game. And that was all that mattered.

•   •   •

The three men who approached the boat were different from the locals who often came up to introduce themselves. We'd met so many kind and supportive folk during the expedition that it was always a surprise on the rare occasion they weren't like that. This was one of those times. This lot certainly didn't want to buy us a beer. Instead, one of them spat on the ground and another called me a British bastard. Wow. What's the problem, mate?

We were now in the marina at Bangor, not far from Belfast. I'd done a stint in Northern Ireland during The Troubles, but I now shared the general impression of most non-Irish people that all that was largely over and Ulster was a far more stable place. A place that was looking forward rather than back. So it was depressing to realise that plenty of the old tensions still seemed to be bubbling just under the surface.

I had no idea where this trio had come from. I suppose it's possible one of them had heard press coverage of the expedition, had maybe even been interested enough to follow me online. Who knows? But they definitely weren't pleased to see me in Bangor.

'A word to the wise,' said one of the friendly locals. 'I'd remove that Union Jack from your cap if I were you.'

'You're serious?' I replied.

'I'm serious,' he said quietly, lowering his voice even though there was nobody to hear him.

Max, Tori, Alfie and Mia were all too young to know that much about The Troubles and were a bit unnerved by the appearance of the three angry men. For my part, I was conscious that we had British military insignia plastered all over our boat as it belonged to the Royal Logistic Corps. My military mind kicked in, of course, and I thought it wise that we should get out of the area as soon as possible in case we became some sort of target, even if for nothing more than unpleasantness and mild aggression.

But before we left, I made a quick trip on my own to Crossmaglen, the dangerous border town where I'd once served. Back then, I had a picture taken of myself carrying a gun as an eighteen-year-old. Now, I took another one on the very same spot, this time holding a paddle. I posted them both online to try to underline the contrast between then and now, nearly twenty years on. A small gesture, of course, but also two fingers to those men on the quayside who clung to the prejudices of the past and who didn't seem to want to accept that positive, peaceful change can be possible.

CHAPTER 15

THE WILD WEST

As I got closer, its image, blurred by both the rain and the hazy light of a November dawn, became slowly sharper, like adjusting the focus of a telescope. It was yet another promontory, another headland, though the local word for that was 'mull'. By this point, of course, I was an old hand at promontories, headlands or whatever. From out at sea, this new one didn't look so very different, the finger of land pointing into the water, the obligatory lighthouse on the clifftop.

Most of the headlands I encountered were impressive, but on a drab morning like this it was hard to see why Paul McCartney had felt moved to write a song about this particular mull. Presumably Macca wrote his lyrics in midsummer, because its romantic charms were not very apparent today. But the Mull of Kintyre was nevertheless significant for me, a landmark in more ways than one, for this was the halfway point of the Great British Paddle. On Day 103, this was, at last, Scotland.

As another old song goes, on a clear day you can see for ever. On a *very* clear day, you can see Scotland from the coast of Northern Ireland. And vice versa; it is said that somebody standing on the tip of the mull can see cars on the Irish coastal roads without the need for binoculars. The stretch of water between the two countries, known as the North Channel, is only 19km across. Not that far to go. Certainly nothing like the challenge posed by getting over from Wales to the Republic of Ireland. On my best days, I'd covered more than twice that.

Except this time I didn't do it the easy way, embarking from the narrowest point of the crossing. The boat and I were still at Bangor Marina when the gauntlet was thrown down. 'Jordan, there's a bloody great weather window all day tomorrow and right through the night too,' said Captain Alex's message. 'If you set out as soon as you can in the morning, you could possibly make it to Scotland in one straight paddle.'

'How far is it?' I asked.

'Nearly 80km.'

'You've got to be kidding?' I said. 'That's four times the shortest route.'

'Yep. But if you don't grab this chance, it'd be a shame. There's no sign of such a fine forecast in the next week or two. What d'you say?'

Surprise, surprise, I picked up the gauntlet. I set off the next morning from the bay of Belfast and achieved a personal best distance of over 77km. I paddled from 1 p.m. till 7.30 a.m. the following day, eighteen and a half hours, at least two thirds of it in darkness. It was a long, long night, but the sea was tolerable for the time of year, and the nearby lights of the boat stopped me feeling too isolated. Despite the comfort of having other people close by, I had to remember to keep a certain distance from the boat, as the turbulence it caused could make the paddle trickier, especially at night, when I couldn't always see the waves coming at me.

There were other things I couldn't see coming at me either. Probably just as well, because this one hit me squarely in the middle of the chest. For a split second, I thought this must be what a heart attack feels like. With a girly scream, I went flying into the water.

'Jesus, what the hell was *that*?' I coughed and spluttered as I surfaced from the icy sea.

Then, by the tiny headlight on my cap, I saw the culprit. A bloody great seagull was sitting on the paddleboard. It looked as dazed as I was, as if it was asking itself exactly the same question... 'What the hell was *that*?'

I wondered what were the statistical chances of being killed in a seagull collision. Certainly quite a stylish way to go. I'd had the idea that our feathered friends had some sort of radar device to avoid such things. Then another notion occurred to me. It is well known that the Scots like a bevvy, but does that apply to their birdlife as well? Was this seagull pissed? It certainly looked as if it needed a bit of a lie down and made no sign of wanting to leave the board. It took a good bit of nudging and yelling before it flew away into the night. Nice to have met you and all that.

Then, rising before me as the darkness lifted came the first sight of the Mull of Kintyre, through a curtain of mist and rain. It was a sight the gloom of which would turn out to be only too prophetic. It had always been the concept of a novice paddler taking on Scotland in the approaching winter which worried people most when they heard about the Great British Paddle, and I was worried too. If I was biting off more than I could chew, the part that threatened to choke me was Scotland – because Scotland was highly likely to bite back.

I was under no illusions. It was well into November now, the days ever shorter, the weather ever less predictable. The west coast of Scotland is arguably the most dramatic part of the British Isles, our equivalent of the Norwegian fjords. Over millennia, the Atlantic Ocean has thrown itself against the land, pummelling it, eroding it, flooding it to create literally hundreds of offshore islands and sea lochs of infinite depth. Come rain or shine, it is a magical, majestic landscape; once seen, never forgotten. Right up there with those fjords. But it is a harsh, unforgiving landscape, where throughout history people had to be strong to survive. And now I was one of that number.

In Scotland, there seemed to be even fewer marinas to shelter and sustain us than in Ireland. The Covid restrictions were tightening their grip all over the country as infection rates began to climb again. From now on, we would need to be ever more careful with both fuel and provisions. We'd even started rationing fresh water; everyone's daily shower was out, and instead the crew had to take dips in the freezing sea. At first, everyone was gung-ho about the idea, but you could see the expressions change on their faces when the water hit certain low-slung parts of the anatomy. I thought of the middle-aged ladies of the Bluetits Chill Swimmers club back in Devon, who could probably have taken this in their stride. Maybe Max, Alfie and me could start a new branch. The Blueballs club.

But the lack of marinas caused another issue too. Sleeping on board the boat at anchor gave us all some very rocky nights, and in my case the consequent chucking-up over the side. Listening to someone else vomiting must be one of the least pleasant experiences in this life, and I always pictured Max, Tori and Alfie pulling their pillows over their ears at the climactic moments.

Bearing in mind my over-sensitised guts, we were dead

careful when passing through the Gulf of Corryvreckan, between the islands of Jura and Scarba in Argyll and Bute. Here, a freakish meeting of totally conflicting tides has created the third largest whirlpool in the world. The gulf is a very beautiful place, with sea eagles flying high above soaring cliffs. Tourists love it, and so far no boat has been lost. Also as yet, nobody has posted an Instagram pic captioned, 'And here we are, just being sucked under by the famous Corryvreckan whirlpool.'

The now familiar pattern of good days and bad days, established so long ago back on the coasts of Dorset and Devon, continued over into Scotland. The 'no paddle days' were in some ways tougher, not just mentally but because we were on a rocky sea and my seasickness was draining me both of fluids and of the vital nutrients I needed to give me the energy to paddle. Increasingly, this became a serious issue with no apparent solution. But the good days were really good, when the sun actually appeared for ten minutes, and I fell in love with the spectacular scenery of Scotland's 'wild west' coastline. The wildlife also became ever more fascinating: sea otters, sea eagles, an osprey and my usual gang of seals and dolphins. On such days, I felt I could have stayed on the water for ever.

Most of the islands of the Inner and Outer Hebrides are linked together by ferry routes operated by the Scottish company Caledonian MacBrayne, universally known as CalMac, and the toots of the horn and the waving from the decks which so often came my way were always a lift to the spirits on a dull grey morning. And nearly every day there was a new island to see. Sometimes large ones that boasted a village or even a small town. Sometimes tiny ones, scarcely more than rocky outcrops, where nobody lived except a farmer and some wind-blown sheep. All of them interesting, all of them beautiful in their different ways.

I certainly fell in love with Tobermory, the main town of the lovely Isle of Mull. Unlike the slightly dour architecture of many Scottish towns, the waterfront of this old fishing port is a parade of houses and shops with facades painted in vivid colours: red, yellow, blue, pink, purple. No shade is too lurid. This gives the buildings an almost Toytown quality, which is why it was the perfect setting for the famous CBeebies series *Balamory*, beloved of a generation of children all over the world.

At Oban, a sad day came for the Great British Paddle team. This was where our first mate Tori Wells had to leave us and return to her usual life. Since she'd joined us back in Wales eight weeks earlier, she'd been a huge support to the expedition, always willing and a fine example of the sort of people the Army Cadet Force attracts to its teams of adult volunteers. Just like me, Tori wanted to make a positive difference to the next generation, and when the school in Djibouti was finally finished there would be a good few bricks bearing her name. She'd been a fantastic crew member, unfazed by living in a cramped space with three sweaty, farty blokes. I really hoped she'd got as much out of her time with us as she'd put into it. She deserved to have a highlander piping her off the boat like some departing admiral, but we couldn't afford that. Still, she went with our grateful thanks and the memory of many happy times together. What a woman!

Tori's departure seemed to really piss off the weather gods, because over the next few days the seas got very much rougher and the temperature dropped like a stone till it was only just above freezing. Even the ladies of the Bluetits Chill Swimmers club might have turned tail and fled. On what was officially the coldest day of the year in Scotland so far, it was finally time for me to open my glamorous wardrobe of water sports gear and haul out the daddy of them all: the drop-dead gorgeous NRS Crux drysuit. This was real top-of-the-range fashion-victim stuff; four layers of waterproof fabric, which stopped water getting in but still allowed moisture like sweat to escape and the skin to breathe properly. The Crux dry-suit was serious gear with an £800 price tag to match, and I looked a bit like something out of *Thunderbirds*. I made a mental note to remember Shaun back in Devon, the kayaker who had forgotten to zip up his flies after taking a leak and nearly drowned. If I made that mistake in the Crux drysuit, I'd probably sink to the bottom faster than the *Titanic*.

Having just lost Tori, the next thing we lost was shore power. For the foreseeable future, the boat would have no heating or hot water – not a cheery prospect as more storms soon came our way and rainy days seemed to become the norm. But still, as always, I grabbed those weather windows, even when they only added 5 or 10km to the total, even when they were in the middle of the sepulchral Scottish night. It always seemed worth it, but all the time I really had to focus on the 'why' of what I was doing, remembering that far away from this freezing sea on a hot, dusty piece of ground in Africa, a building was rising. Remembering too the face of little Ibrahim, whose dream was to go to school. And on I paddled.

And the occasional good day could still produce pretty good mileage. Some 24km one day; 37km the next. Eventually, we reached the Isle of Skye, going under the soaring bridge that now links the island with mainland Scotland. It was the first and only bridge I had to go under on the Great British Paddle, and Alfie made sure to film this thrilling moment. Reaching Skye was good news, because for a few days at least this large island would hopefully act as a barrier between us and the worst of the Atlantic weather systems. More knights in shining armour appeared on the horizon too, in the shape of two paddleboard experts, David and William, who offered to fill up our gas canisters. Since the boat now wasn't allowed to dock anywhere due to Covid, I had to paddle to the shore with the empty canisters and return with the full ones, which was undoubtedly the slowest paddle of the entire expedition.

In succession to my infected leg and my seasickness, I developed a brand-new problem: an ache in my side that got so sore I was forced to curtail several paddles due to the pain. At first, I assumed this was just the latest of the countless aches and pains my poor body now suffered. I didn't allow myself to think it might be anything worse, as there was a slight shortage of A&E departments in this neck of the woods. It certainly wasn't the best location in which to be seriously ill. I crossed my fingers and tried to rest my body as much as possible; not a great experience on an unheated boat on a rough sea with the rain pissing down. Now and again, my mind would drift back to the life of luxury I'd so often led in my maritime security days. The five-star hotels, the swimming pools, the waiters coming to the sun lounger with a tray of drinks. I reminded myself sharply that I'd chosen to give up that sort of life to do something a bit more worthwhile. It usually worked, but sometimes it was a struggle.

The weather forecast remained dire. Rarely now was there that old tension-making discrepancy between Captain Alex's gloomy forecasts and the reality on the spot. Alex told us it would be shit, and it almost always was. Glimpses of sunlight were as rare as hens' teeth. And yet, even in such conditions, the scenery of western Scotland could still be mesmerising in its rugged savagery. Rain and wind couldn't dent its visual impact, and in an odd way they could even add to it. The further north we went, the more bare and primeval the landscape became. There were fewer wooded slopes and lush pastures; this was nature stripped down to its essentials. On Day 128 of the Great British Paddle, as November turned into December and meteorological winter officially began, Max, Alfie and I went up on deck to find that the *Spirit of St George II* looked slightly different. Sort of, well, paler. Once we'd wiped the sleep from our eyes, it was clear what it was: for the first time, the boat was covered in frost and snow. It would turn out to be the worst Scottish winter in a decade. Scotland really was biting back.

• • •

Not far in front of us another great headland was looming, one that not even Paul McCartney had ever considered writing a song about. This wasn't a cuddly place. Nor did it have a cuddly name. That would have been quite ridiculous. It was called Cape Wrath.

Now I even felt sick on the paddleboard. Before this, being

on the board had actually been an escape from the nausea, but now even that compensation was torn from me. Yet, in some perverse way, that almost made me more determined to carry on. Let the weather do its worst; I would stay in the game.

Max, Alfie and I had by now decided that there were three types of 'fun' on the Great British Paddle. Type 1 was when it really was fun. Type 2 was when you thought it was miserable at the time, but in retrospect you realised that it wasn't really that bad. Type 3 was when it was, in fact, total sodding misery. Right now, most of our fun was Type 3. Sometimes, when I climbed back on the boat after a paddle, I was shivering so much I simply couldn't stop. Scotland wasn't just biting back, it seemed to want to devour me whole. Distracted by its beauty, I simply hadn't counted on its brutality.

For the first time, the close resemblance of a paddleboard to a surfboard, essentially totally different disciplines, actually had some substance. Instead of avoiding the waves as much as possible, I tried to embrace them, and it worked. Quite often, if the wind was behind me, I found that I was actually able to ride the waves and make progress that way. Though I was extremely careful, it was a slightly dangerous technique, and I often landed in the water. But the kilometres mounted up and that was always the name of the game.

And every day, the spectre of Cape Wrath was getting a

little bit closer. I'll not pretend it didn't scare me. The Lizard and Land's End in August were nursery slopes compared to this. So, it was an inspiration to discover I wasn't the only paddleboarder in the village. One day, almost literally, I bumped into a man called Charlie Head, who was on a similar mission to myself; in his case, he was circumnavigating the coast of Scotland. He and I were going in opposite directions, so it was very useful for both of us to be told what perils we could both expect on our different journeys. Charlie was yet another campaigner trying to raise awareness of mental health. It always gave me such satisfaction to realise how much was being done in this context. Not many years ago, it was something swept under the carpet, hushed up, denied even, especially among men who were suffering from anxiety, depression and other mental health problems. It was all that macho crap again, all that stiff upper lip bollocks. Men must hide their feelings. Men must butch up and carry on. And men certainly didn't cry. What me, Charlie Head, Sally Orange and so many others were trying to get across was that even the most apparently strong and sorted people can be prone to such difficulties, and it is never a weakness to reach out for help but a strength.

•   •   •

Under Max Rivers's commitment and guidance, the *Spirit of St George II* had now reached the relative safety of the tiny port of Kinlochbervie on the north-western tip of the county of Sutherland. It's just a harbour, a small village and not much else, but they kindly allowed us to moor. Behind Kinlochbervie rose some unforgettable scenery. At first glance, you'd have called them mountains, but that wasn't quite accurate. Up here, they are called 'stacks': huge outcrops of almost barren rock that rise out of the landscape like great behemoths from another age. Beautiful maybe wasn't quite the word; they were too awesome for that. But for me the big attraction at Kinlochbervie was the unexpected existence of a medical centre, which served the surrounding isolated communities. The aching pain in my side hadn't got any better. I'd already managed to get some medical advice over the phone from Dr Rome Begum back in Andover, and from my symptoms it hadn't been considered that anything serious was going on. That was a relief from worry but not from the bloody pain, which refused to disappear, and I was glad to get a proper touchy-feely examination. 'You've been putting your body through a unique experience,' the medic said. 'It's not very happy, but it's coping as best it can.'

That made sense. Of course my body wasn't happy. It had been telling me that since the very first week on the board. I guess by this stage it was whimpering for mercy and begging me to take it home. There were certainly days when I longed to obey. One night, just after I'd spoken to my little girl on the phone, the emotional price of the expedition finally got through my defences and hit me hard. I would have given anything to be with her, but I forced that thought to the back of my mind.

I was getting closer and closer to completing the whole left-hand side of mainland Great Britain, but the mighty Cape Wrath refused to let me get anywhere near. For several days, we sat on the boat waiting for a window. As soon as there was one, I headed out to sea, even though there were some seriously big swells, much too high for me to employ my new surfing technique. Nevertheless, I made it 26km towards the cape, but the shortness of the day meant I lost the light, and it was just too dodgy to carry on. Damn and blast. But by now, I'd learnt that to conquer this landscape you just had to keep on the attack. You had to get back into the battle if you wanted to win the war. OK, I'd just lost this one, but I was determined to get round the damn cape the next time.

In the meantime, it was back to Kinlochbervie and to another three days twiddling my thumbs, wanting to throw up and waiting for the next window. It came, and eventually I got round the notorious Cape Wrath. In some ways, it was the northern equivalent of the white cliffs of Dover, even though the cliffs here were slate-grey. It gave off that same impression of a mighty, impregnable bastion, a natural bulwark against invasion. It must have given the Norsemen pause for thought, though clearly not enough to stop them raping and pillaging people on the west coast of Scotland for several centuries.

As an early Christmas present, Daz now returned to the boat for the next leg of the Great British Paddle. He'd been relieved of his army duties for the Christmas period and decided to join us for a while so Max could spend the holiday season with his family. Max had done a brilliant job of captaining the boat in really tough conditions. He'd been a pro to his fingertips and deserved a break. After all, I'd just been steering a paddleboard; Max had been steering a 40ft yacht.

But when we made our farewells, I struggled to hide my envy behind the usual jokes and boys' banter. This would be the first Christmas in her life when I would not see my daughter. Kids are resilient, and I knew Evie would cope, but I knew too that she would be sad; the fathers of her school friends would all be at their firesides. It would also have been wonderful to see my mum and dad, and Megan too. I could picture them all in their various houses doing the corny Christmas stuff, and I'd be stuck here on this bloody boat. And if I had to throw up, it would've been a lot nicer if the cause was turkey, sprouts and roast potatoes followed by Christmas pudding with clotted cream and way too many beers. As 25 December approached, I had to remind myself again and again that this had been my choice.

The boat had now left Kinlochbervie, and it began to follow me again. Having passed Cape Wrath, we turned right along the northern coast of Scotland, heading for John O'Groats. Now there was nothing between us and Iceland, and it was bitter. The training I'd done the previous year for my series of marathons in cold climates had taught me a lot about how the body deals with cold. But that had been about coping with relatively short bursts of freezing temperatures – an hour in a cryo-chamber; a day-long marathon in Siberia or Yukon followed by a good meal and a long kip in a cosy bed. This was different. This was cold as a form of torture. A relentless, rain-soaked, never-ending misery that would wear you down if you allowed it to. The mental struggle was to stop that happening. The best defence against it was the camaraderie among the three of us. Daz kept the black humour going most of the time, and Alfie, as well as shooting some stunning video footage of Scottish seascapes, behaved with a cool maturity that belied his youth.

But the windows for paddling were becoming smaller and smaller. Whenever a sliver of brightness did poke through for an hour, we greeted it in awe like ancient worshippers of the sun gods. And yet, when it did and some progress was made, that old blue therapy was still there, still potent. The battlements of cliffs, which could look almost malevolent beneath sheets of rain, seemed to lighten in colour and become almost beautiful. The sea too would change out of its usual grey drabness and put on pretty shades of pale blue and green. But such times were increasingly rare. And still new and unexpected hazards came rolling our way, a major one being the coastal entrance to a sea loch called Loch Eriboll, the presence of which created a wind tunnel off the sea that was almost impossible to cross over. A struggle every metre of the way.

I began to feel that we were almost at a standstill. The windows had now shrunk to the size of portholes, and a passable day's paddling was starting to look like a major event, when I almost felt we should send fireworks into the sky. The boat was still unheated, and on the long, inactive days with nothing much to do except keep our online presence alive and kicking, it could almost feel like a floating prison. At these bleak times, it was often a lifesaver that I could talk to Paula Reid about my physical and emotional state. Every time, she somehow managed to reboot my spirits and transform the Moaning Minnie with the aching knees and the pain in his side back into an extreme adventurer who just wasn't going to give up whatever challenges were thrown at him next. As I've noted before, so many extreme adventurers are people with military backgrounds who have found that civilian life lacks the stimulus and excitement the services provide. And so, often it is the discipline and commitment that is such a big part of military training that keeps you going. The big difference between the two ways of life is that in the military, you always have a commanding officer telling you what to do; in civilian life, nobody is doing that. Nobody is your commanding officer except you.

As the *Spirit of St George II* rocked on the wintry seas, as I tried to stay warm and forget that it was Christmas, I repeated in my head my command to myself from five months before: 'Orders to Corporal Wylie of the King's Royal Hussars: you will circumnavigate Great Britain on a paddleboard in order to raise enough money to build a school in Africa.'

Perfectly clear. No room for doubt there. A job to be done; let's get on with it. They say John O'Groats is lovely at this time of year.

CHAPTER 16

NICOLA SAYS NO

The end, when it came, was swift and final. Nicola Sturgeon said no. Or, to be precise, some minion in the office of the First Minister of Scotland did. It was said very courteously, expressing admiration for what the Great British Paddle was trying to achieve and regret that the present exceptional circumstances should interfere with it. But everyone's lives were being messed up right now and there was no reason why we should be exempt. In an official email we pleaded our case, pointing out that three blokes on a boat at sea were hardly likely to spread the infection and outlining the precautions we took when we were in harbour. But it was no good. If we continued, we would be in breach of the tighter restrictions just about to come into force. The Veterans Minister at the time, Johnny Mercer MP, also a former army commando who had become a good friend, did his best to help us as he had tried to fight our corner all the way round, but unfortunately it just wasn't to be.

We set up a Zoom call with Captain Alex, Paula and other members of the core team. Yes, we could go on arguing with the Scottish government but that seemed like a straw in the wind. We could even ignore the email for a day or two and hope that an unexpected weather window might give me the time to cover those 23km to John O'Groats, the place at which I would have established a new world first. But the feeling was strong in everyone that we should do the right thing and not diminish the expedition by being bolshie and combative with a government that had so much on its plate. For the past 150 days, we had followed every rule and regulation in the maritime rule book and shown respect to everyone we'd come across, even the grumpy fishermen. Why behave any differently now? So, that was it. The Great British Paddle was over. At least for the time being. That email from the Scottish government wasn't much of a Christmas present.

That's not to say we were totally selfless and noble about it. Everyone was down in the dumps, and I, of course, was gutted. Only 23 bloody kilometres to set that record. Yet, I'd always been crystal clear in my own mind that this wasn't about records for me but raising the money to build a school. At this moment, for the thousandth time, I had to remember my 'why'.

The axe had fallen on the Great British Paddle at a place called Scrabster, near Thurso on the Caithness coast. Scrabster is the port from which ferries ply across to Orkney and is a pretty bleak location in midwinter. Sad to say, the courtesy we'd received from the Scottish government hadn't been duplicated by some of the people who'd crossed our path in the past few days. The harbour master at Scrabster seemed to regard us as a trio of frivolous airheads causing extra bother at a time when there was more than enough bother to go around. The fact we had a worthwhile cause seemed to cut no ice with him at all.

But it was worse than that. He waved an email in our faces from the local MP, condemning our expedition and demanding it be stopped. How this MP had been alerted to us is an interesting question. Though we can't prove it, we were all pretty sure somebody with a grudge against us had been doing their best to stymie the Great British Paddle. Who knows what that grudge might have been – and there's little to be gained from speculating – but something similarly suspicious had happened a few weeks ago, just after we'd reached Scotland. Somebody trying to cause us trouble. And now, at Scrabster, it was possibly happening again. It was a depressing thought that, presumably knowing the reason for the expedition, somebody was bitter and twisted enough to want to kill it. So that was when we'd emailed the Scottish government, and Nicola said no.

It was now 23 December. We'd been facing the slightly grim prospect of Christmas without our families, and suddenly that was no longer necessary, so, after 150 days, the Great British Paddle was wound up with astonishing speed. It was arranged that the boat would be moored at Scrabster until Daz's superiors at the Royal Logistic Corps could arrange for its removal. The £600 worth of provisions we'd only just stocked up were given away to local charities. Alfie's family rushed up from Glasgow to pick him up and take him home, and Max, who had literally just returned that same day, hired a van to take him and me back down south. Suddenly, we were going to have family Christmases after all. Inside the thick black cloud of disappointment, that was the great big silver lining, and everyone's emotions were spinning round like washing in a dryer.

The news that the Great British Paddle had come to an end had now broken on social media, and the messages poured in. From our families and friends. From many of those who had helped us out since 26 July: the B&Bs, the hotels, the lovely people with spare bedrooms, the pubs that had given us meals. From everyone who'd supported us along the way: paddleboarders and kayakers who had ridden with me for a bit, the lifeboat stations that had given us so much advice.

And from all those people I'd never met and never would, who had been excited and enthused by the whole crazy thing.

Naturally, the overwhelming tone of the messages was disappointment and sympathy, though liberally laced with praise for having got this far. I had to stop reading them after a while. In a sense, it was best that way. I'd answer many of them in a while, but not just yet.

And then, as we packed our kit and got ready to close up the boat, something wonderful happened on that bleak quayside at Scrabster. Out of the grey December afternoon, a group of people materialised and headed towards us, mostly youngsters with a few adults tagging behind. It was a contingent from the local branch of the Army Cadet Force and some of their parents. Instead of staying warm indoors or buying last-minute Christmas presents, they'd taken the trouble to come to wave us off. It was a moving gesture, and my tears were pretty damn close. For the umpteenth time, I felt so proud to be associated with the Army Cadet Force for turning out young people like these. No doubt they spent endless hours on their phones, but at least they weren't blinded to the wider world. All those phones were out, of course, snapping away furiously, but I hoped that if they did use Photoshop later, they'd include me in that process because by this point I certainly needed tarting up. Max, Alfie and I were so grateful that they'd come. Their presence changed a moment which, however much I told myself otherwise, naturally carried a slight sense of failure into a powerful moment of real achievement.

In the gloomy harbour at Scrabster, this gang of kids and their parents were to be the last wonderful personification of all the fantastic people I'd encountered since I paddled out of Essex Marina 150 days ago. On that fine July morning, my friend Pat, the chaplain, had blessed me and the expedition. And it came to me now that his blessing had worked, in so many different ways. The Great British Paddle had brought me so much that I would always treasure: spectacular images of the sea and the coast that I would carry with me for ever and memories of so much kindness from strangers.

• • •

Max and I drove south in the hired van. In the back was all my kit, and of course the board and the paddle. It had felt strange putting them into the van and seeing them lying there, lifeless objects. It might sound daft, but for the past 150 days it had seemed to me that the board and paddle were almost like living things, almost like extra limbs of my own body: the board an extension of my feet, the paddle of my hands. Now, they lay beached in the dark interior of the van when they should have been out on the sunlit water where they belonged. Dancing over the waves, challenging the winds and the tides, as much part of sea life as the gulls and the cormorants, the seals and the dolphins.

As we headed down through the Highlands until we reached the motorway network that would speed us southwards, it felt weird travelling on four wheels again on a hard, unmoving surface. I had become so used to the world shifting constantly beneath me that it felt almost unnatural when it didn't. I wondered what it was going to be like once again being part of what my GP in Andover had termed the 'real world'. I wondered how I'd cope, how easy my re-entry would be. Because I'd not been prepared for this sudden, dramatic change of circumstance. Had Covid and/or the Scottish winter weather not stopped me, I'd have spent the next sixty to seventy days paddling down the east coast of the British Isles. And though in January and February it would hardly have been a doddle, it was unlikely to have been as challenging as the bad-tempered Irish Sea or the wild west of Scotland. By the time I was due to see the Thames Estuary once again, the daffodils would have been out along the banks of the River Crouch, waving their yellow heads to welcome me back into Essex Marina. That was a scene I had often pompously pictured in my head. The crowds lining the shore, the flags, the bunting, the brass band even. It'd be like Drake returning from the defeat of the Spanish Armada or Nelson after the Battle of the Nile. Ha ha. Dream on, Jordan. Dial it down. And yet, on so many wet, lonely, dark nights out on the board, I had indeed imagined some sort of victorious return to the River Crouch. Job done. Record broken. More than enough money raised for the school in Djibouti. Now, of course, that just wasn't going to happen.

After a sixteen-hour drive through the wintry night, Max dropped me off at my house in Andover before heading home to the Isle of Wight. It was tough saying goodbye to him; even tougher feeling that the team, which had kept me afloat in every sense of the word for the past 150 days, was now dissolving. As Max turned his van around and drove off down the lane, I put the familiar key into the familiar lock and entered my cold, empty house. I fell into my bed, chilly and unaired but luxurious compared to my cabin on the boat, and slept like a baby. It was the morning of Christmas Eve.

By now, most people in my life knew what had happened from social media, and my ex-partner Laura had invited me to her home for Christmas lunch. But Evie didn't know I was back, and they had been trying to keep her away from social media so that my return would be a total surprise. And though I didn't have presents for anyone, it didn't matter. I myself was to be the present for Evie. When she saw me, she couldn't believe it, and neither could I. Just forty-eight hours ago, I'd been on that boat in Scrabster Harbour facing the end of the Great British Paddle. But that amazed hug from my little girl was the best thing Santa could ever have brought me. It still gave me a pang to see my child being brought up under someone else's roof, and that would probably never change, but I always tried to remember that I bore a huge part of the responsibility for this outcome, and as time went by it gradually became a little easier.

And it seemed that Santa had decided to be extra kind to me that Christmas, because later that day, after the turkey and the pudding, he paid me a second visit. This time, he came down the chimney not as a fat, hairy old bloke in a red jumpsuit but in the highly glamorous shape of my great friend Kay Burley. Kay had always been a great supporter of my adventures in the past; she's been like a big sister to me, and, as I've written, she had given regular and generous coverage to the Great British Paddle on Sky News all the way along. And now, on Christmas Day, she did something that was way beyond generous. Invited to appear on the Christmas celebrity edition of ITV quiz programme *The Chase*, Kay had chosen our Frontline Children charity as the good cause she was there to fight for. And hey, what d'you know, the lady won. Yep, she actually won more than anyone had won before, and the £50,000 prize money came to us. To say this was a boost to the coffers at exactly the point when it was urgently needed is a massive understatement. I watched the TV in utter disbelief, my jaw hitting the ground, my heart rate going through the roof. It was a totally incredible feeling. Like when a piece of film is played at high speed, I had a sudden mental picture of that school building at As Eyla – the bricks flying onto the walls, the glass appearing in the window frames, the tiles slamming down onto the roofs like stamps on a letter. As far as I'm concerned, Kay Burley is Mother Teresa of Calcutta and Saint Bernadette of Lourdes rolled into one. I'm thinking of building a little shrine – a nice framed photo of Kay, candles and incense, spiritual music on a constant loop, the whole shebang. I can never thank her enough.

Miraculously, Kay's gesture seemed to be the gift that kept on giving, because her generosity seemed unlock the same response in others. Maybe the British were just more moved by an attempt that didn't quite come off than they would have been by one that succeeded. Maybe they all felt sorry for me. I don't know. I don't care. All I know is that there was an instant tsunami of donations, which lifted our total to around £90,000. A bit still to be raised, but enough to pretty much guarantee that the building at As Eyla would be completed. Little Ibrahim and all those other kids were going to get their school.

●   ●   ●

Guess what happened next – no prizes, though. My re-entry to the 'real world' was harder than I imagined it might be. After those 150 tumultuous days on the ironing board, after the huge disappointment of having to abandon the challenge immediately followed by the euphoria of the money rolling in, my mental health crashed again. Maybe it had all been too much of an emotional roller-coaster. Logically, I should have been euphoric. In a few months, Covid permitting, I would be getting on a plane and going to Djibouti to see the school full of children, the dream fulfilled. How awesome would that be. I was back near my beloved daughter again, and I was really keen to rekindle my embryonic relationship with the lovely Megan, who had been so patient during the expedition. Nor was I short of things to do. There was still plenty of admin connected with Frontline Children, and I'd also started to focus on my next adventure, which was going to be my long-delayed marathons in the Arctic and the Antarctic. I'd also started the process of writing this book, which is always a big adventure in itself. So, who knows why, throughout the usual bleakness of a British January, I began to hear the black dog growling in the distance? And before too long, he was right back snapping at my heels.

Maybe it was a withdrawal symptom from blue therapy, that treatment which had had such a transformative effect on me for those 150 days. For all that time, my horizons had been infinite, the sky my roof and the sea my floor. Now, I was back to the conventional ceiling and four walls. Despite the miserable cold days and all the throwing up over the side, I missed it. I found myself moping on the sofa, picturing the seals and the dolphins, the crowd on the cliff at Land's End, the Army Cadet Force kids who'd come to the quayside at Scrabster. I'd remember the smell of the sea, the feel of the sun on my face, the pure clean air blowing away any negativity in my mind. During the paddle, I'd managed to convince myself I would never need the medication again, that somehow the Great British Paddle had 'cured' me once and for all. But now I could see that I was wrong. Shit.

Of course, it wasn't just personal stuff that was causing it. All over the world, people were going through terrible, unprecedented times. In the UK, the second wave of Covid was hitting hard; far worse than the first. Hundreds were dying every day. The hospitals were struggling to cope. The economy was taking a massive hit, and millions lived in fear of losing their jobs and their homes. And it was winter. A perfect storm. Spring seemed a long way off.

Still, though, I didn't want to admit defeat and put myself back on the pills. To use the obvious paddleboarding metaphor, I was struggling with my balance, wobbling dangerously, and no matter how skilfully I paddled I was soon going to fall in. After a few weeks, that's exactly what happened – and there was a pretty big splash. I even needed a couple of days in hospital to be professionally looked after so they could get me back onto an even keel. When I was handed the glass of water and the first pills I'd taken in nearly six months, I had a tangle of feelings. A big part of me still didn't want to give in, but another part of me just wanted to feel better. So, I took the pills, and after a time I did begin to feel better. Close friends were supportive as ever. Laura was brilliant; despite the break-up of our relationship, we'd stayed close and still cared about each other's happiness. But, as the old saying goes, a boy's best friend is his mother, and now mine came down from Blackpool to help me convalesce. For most of the time, I stayed in bed and slept constantly while Mum pottered around downstairs, doing the housework and trying to make me eat something when I woke. She was always there, but she never intruded when she sensed I wanted to be left alone. And even when I felt that way, there was a deep comfort in knowing she was near and would come if I called, just as she had done when I was sick in bed as a kid. There's a primeval connection between parent and child that never goes away, whether you're a five-year-old with the measles or a 35-year-old extreme adventurer with anxiety and depression. Sometimes, when the moment was right, she'd sit on the end of my bed and we'd have long talks. No doubt she struggled to understand my mental health problems; one minute paddling round Cape Wrath in a howling gale, the next huddled under the duvet in Andover. But so much about mental health is indeed hard, impossible maybe, for those not afflicted to understand. Christ, even those who suffer from it have the same difficulty. But the bottom line is that my mother was there for me yet again, just as she had been when I found myself on that rooftop in Dubai.

Slowly, the pretty pills did their work, and despite my previous rejection of psychotherapy, I had another few sessions, and this time round I got much more out of it. Gradually, the barking of the black dog receded again, and I faced up to the fact that I was still going to need the pills for the foreseeable future. I felt no shame in that, only disappointment that it was necessary. Nevertheless, I still hope that I won't need them for ever. It wasn't that blue therapy had failed me. Quite the opposite; it had been a revelation. It was just that, at this point in my life, it hadn't been quite enough on its own. So, I'm still on my journey towards complete healing. With the valuable insights I've gained from therapy, I'm going to go on circumnavigating myself on a sort of mental paddleboard, and I feel sure that one day I'm going to reach my destination.

CHAPTER 17

KEEPING MY PROMISE

It's a funny feeling, waking up to what you know is going to be a day you'll never forget. A day that when you're old and grey and nearing the end of the road will be one of the memories that you reach out for and relive as if it were yesterday. Obviously that day will start like any other. You get out of bed, shower and shave, brush your teeth, eat breakfast and do all the normal things. But you know that by the time you climb back into bed that night, something amazing will have taken place.

That was what happened to me on the morning of Friday 14 May 2021. The sounds outside my window were not the ones I was used to. Like the postman shoving letters through the box. My neighbours' cars starting up as they went off to work. The trains on the nearby line streaking past on their way to London or wherever. Now, I was a long way from Andover. I was an even longer way from the stormy seas of northern Scotland. Outside this window, postmen and trains were thin on the ground. What I could hear were the sounds of Africa. The birds in the trees, the braying of a donkey, the cackling of chickens; the noises of a farm waking up. And it was a beautiful morning. Already warm and promising to be another baking-hot day in Djibouti. I'd made it. I'd got here. I could hardly believe it.

But getting here hadn't been easy. Even now, right up to the last, it seemed that fate wanted to throw obstacles in my way. Luckily, compared to those I'd already faced on the paddleboard, they were minor pinpricks. Still irritating, though. The moment the ban on international travel from the UK had been relaxed a little, I'd tried to get my bum on a plane to Djibouti. It had taken some nifty footwork, but I'd managed to get a flight to Turkey, and from there I could fly onwards to Djibouti. But literally as I sat in the plane on the Heathrow runway, a text came through from the airline to tell me that Turkey had been placed on the 'red list' of Covid countries, and my return ticket from Istanbul would no longer be valid. So how the hell would I get back home? Sod it. I was going to Djibouti and that was that. I'd work out the rest later.

At As Eyla, the school was pretty much ready. I'd picked up from my contacts on the ground that the building was already in partial use. The teachers and the kids had sneaked in before it was totally finished, the very moment it was possible to do so. I think they were trying to hide this fact in case I was hurt they'd not waited for me to get there, but I didn't mind in the least. In fact, I was moved that they just couldn't wait to get started; it only underlined just how much the school was needed.

Just before I left the UK, right at the last moment, another of those wonderful acts of generosity that had so often kept me going came my way. A local Andover company called Stitch A Logo, run by Caroline and Neil Dyke, offered to supply me with 100 school uniforms and 100 school bags. I said, 'Yes, please' but that I was flying in less than forty-eight hours. Amazingly, these great people worked through the night to deliver the gear. They even threw in twelve footballs and some marker cones for use on a football pitch. Such generosity and selflessness. The human race can be pretty bloody wonderful sometimes – but at other times, sadly not. At Istanbul, Turkish Airlines showed no generosity at all, no matter how much I explained that all this excess baggage was for charitable reasons. The poker-faced customs officials had no interest in hearing about my worthy cause and slapped me with $400 worth of duties. Miserable sods, the lot of them. I suppressed a strong urge to ram one of the football cones where the sun didn't shine.

It was wonderful to look down from the plane and see the Mediterranean give way to the coastline of Africa, all so familiar to me for so many years now. Then down the length of the Suez Canal towards the Bab el-Mandeb Strait and the Gate of Tears, which I'd rowed across a year and a half before in the adventure that had seeded the idea of the Great British Paddle. Soon, I could see the familiar shark-fin shape of Ras Sayan, the mountain which had been my lighthouse on that dangerous voyage. My God, what a lot had happened since then. The marathons in Siberia, Yukon, Alaska and Iceland. The earth-shattering impact of Covid. The misery of the lockdowns.

Even at Djibouti, they slapped me with $100 in import taxes. No point in explaining the purpose of my visit or trying to drop the name of the Minister of Education; all they could see was shiny new goods which I might try to sell in some street market. Hey-ho. Easier to pay up and shut up. It was great to see Djibouti City once again, but my driver, an old friend of over ten years called Loubak who was a local fixer/agent/man of many parts, was waiting to take me straight off on the four-hour drive out to As Eyla.

Jesus, I'd almost forgotten how rough that road was. Overturned trucks and potholes as big as craters on the moon. As always, the poverty I glimpsed along the way brought back home the relative privilege that most people in the West, Covid or no Covid, are able to enjoy. There were no motorway services here. No M&S, no KFC, no W. H. Smith. If you wanted to poo in these parts, you went behind a tree. If there was one. Or if you could be bothered.

Our destination was an unusual billet close to the village of As Eyla, a neem farm named after the species of tree which is the basis for many of the products used in Ayurvedic medicine. The farm called itself an agro-forestry regeneration project dedicated to sustainability, and it took in paying guests to help its finances. It was a simple but beautiful place, an oasis in the surrounding barren land. Many Westerners might have found it basic, but in this neck of the woods it was like staying at The Ritz.

The moment of first seeing the school was of course a big deal. Plenty of photographs had been sent to me over the past year as the buildings had slowly risen from the ground. But standing there and seeing it in reality was a different ball game. I could throw a load of superlative adjectives at you here, but I won't. I reckon you can guess anyway.

The opening ceremony took place the morning after I arrived at 9 o'clock sharp. School bell time. But I doubt it was much like the opening of any new school in the UK. This was almost like a carnival. Music was pumping out and people came dressed in bright colours. There was a sense of positivity and joy in the air that you could almost breathe in. It was comically clear that, as suspected, the school had been up and running for a good few weeks, and this jamboree was totally for my benefit. I wasn't complaining.

All the tribal leaders from the village came out to meet me, the chief in his traditional outfit. Communication was difficult, even with Loubak my driver chum translating, but their faces spoke loudly of how pleased they were. As Eyla had never had any sort of nursery or primary school before, and as well as the teachers, other jobs had been created too: security men, cleaners, cooks etc. The new school was a big deal for this village in the middle of nowhere.

The local people wanted to name the school after me, but I wasn't comfortable with that, so I encouraged them to give it a name that resonated with the locals. As a nod to local cultural and political sensitivities, the Djibouti government decided to name it after one of the tribal leaders in the area. And so, the school now bears the title Garderie Sultan Houmed Loita. And that's just fine by me.

The moment I cut the ribbon to declare the school formally open was pretty emotional, though I managed not to blub. Naturally, it was the moment that made everything worthwhile. Every frozen toe and finger, the chattering teeth, the jellyfish stings, the infected leg, the paddling alone in the pitch dark, the endless dunkings in a ball-freezing sea, the throwing-up every five minutes. All those times when I'd not been sure I could handle much more were far behind me. All those times I'd yearned to go home to see my own child and sleep in my own cosy bed were forgotten about. All of it vanished on the breeze at the sight of those little kids smiling and laughing and just so happy to be in that school. Now it felt like the hardships I'd put myself through hadn't really been hardships at all; they'd been privileges.

After cutting the ribbon, I raised the flag of our Frontline Children charity to flutter alongside the Djibouti national standard and unveiled a plaque on the wall that had my name on it. One of the proudest and most fulfilling moments of my life.

Only the first 100 children were there that day; the others would follow later. And plenty of parents were there too, everyone excited. The Djibouti government had decreed that it was to be an early years school for children aged from about four to seven years. In this very patriarchal society, I was very pleased to see that at least 50 per cent were girls. The kids lined up eagerly to get their school uniforms, which was essentially a polo shirt with the school's name and logo on it. Their thrill at getting such a simple gift was touching, a sharp reminder that children in a UK school would never have shown remotely the same enthusiasm.

Though not up to the standard of a newly built British school, the buildings were modern and sophisticated. The six classrooms were air-conditioned, and the electricity was powered by solar panels. There were also new toilets, and shower facilities and living quarters for the teachers.

After the ceremony, I visited the kids in their various classrooms and tried to engage with them as best I could, teaching them to count to ten in English and to sing that old children's song 'Heads, shoulders, knees and toes', which transcends any language barrier. Great fun. Through an interpreter, I tried to tell them a bit about how I'd raised the money for the school, talking about my adventures rowing across the Gate of Tears, running cold-climate marathons and doing the Great British Paddle, even if they didn't fully understand some of it. They'd never lived in a cold climate or seen snow; they'd probably never seen the sea either and had certainly never heard of anything called a paddleboard. I showed them some of James May's and Alfie Marsh's videos on my phone, and it was great to see all these little eyes grow wide with amazement on glimpsing wider worlds.

Broadening horizons is surely what education is all about. And yet it was also clear that the world of this small school was in itself a huge improvement on the barren landscape and war-torn existence most of them knew outside its gates. Once again, it was brought back to me forcibly how basic were the lives of these people in this remote, sun-baked landscape. The adults had to work hard for low pay as farm labourers or camel-herders; the children had to pitch in to keep the families afloat, washing clothes by the side of the road and fetching and carrying buckets of water. Forced to be grown up before their time, their childhoods were very far from those enjoyed by most kids in Britain. It was simply another planet.

The six teachers had come from the city, with their relocation funded by the government. Life in the middle of nowhere would be a massive change for these folk, and the pay wasn't exactly great, but they were young and dedicated men and women who wanted to make a positive difference to the future of their country. They were keen to show me that this wasn't going to be some inferior school giving only the most rudimentary learning to its pupils; it would be somewhere they would learn mathematics, literacy and many of the skills that could transform their prospects in later life. Even English was to be taught for an hour a week. I found these young teachers inspirational. Education was their passion. Good on them. Respect.

I'd return to the school several times during the next week or so. I suppose I hoped that at least some of these kids might remember me as a person, not just as the name on the plaque they would pass by every day but never look at. Every time I went back, I enjoyed it more. Because here, right in front of me and written in capital letters, was my 'reason why'. It was written on a small smiling face or in a high five, in the joy brought by the wearing of the new polo shirts or in the proud ownership of pens and pencils. Seeing the reason why so brilliantly brought to life was far more wonderful than I'd imagined it might be. As that Blackpool boy who had so undervalued his own education, I hoped I had now made up a little for that unintended sin.

On that day of the opening ceremony, in the midst of the music, the snipping of ribbons and all the lovely fuss, I constantly tried to scan the sea of faces for one I would recognise. But I could never spot it. So, where was Ibrahim?

•   •   •

For days I walked around the village looking for him, hoping to see his face in the crowd, but I never did. I imagined he must have known about the school, so why wasn't he at the ceremony? Why wasn't he in one of the classrooms? I didn't know his second name, only his first, and I guessed Ibrahim was a very common name around here. Eventually, with Loubak interpreting, we went to the tribal leader whom I'd met on the big day and showed him the photo of the boy and me which had been taken three years before. 'I know this boy,' he said at once. 'Come on, I'll take you to him.'

We jumped into a car and ten minutes later arrived at one of the clay-built shacks that passed for houses. A woman came out. She looked about ninety, though she might not have been much more than middle-aged. At first, she wasn't very friendly at all. She started shouting and gesticulating and didn't seem to grasp the simple reason for our arrival. Her bark was worse than her bite, but still we didn't get very far till I pulled out the photo again. At once her attitude entirely changed. She looked ten years younger. She even hugged me – an astonishing action between an Arab woman and a Western man who had never met. I have no idea what thoughts were passing through her mind as she called out towards the hut.

A small figure came out. A little taller, maybe about seven or eight now, but unmistakeably him. At first, he didn't recognise me. At that age, three years is a very long time. So yet again I brought out the photograph. At once, a big smile lit up Ibrahim's face as the memory returned to him. He threw himself at me and began to cry. And the emotion I'd managed to keep in check at the opening ceremony got the better of me now.

It was hard to get a clear picture of his life these days. When I'd known him before, he'd been in the orphanage with his two older sisters, but now it seemed as if this toothless old woman had taken him in. She was old enough to be his grandmother, but no doubt such considerations just didn't matter in this situation. Anyway, good on her.

I showed him some of the other photos of us that I had stored on my phone. I sensed that he was overwhelmed that somebody cared enough about him to keep his picture for such a long time.

'Why isn't Ibrahim at the school?' I asked my driver. But even as the words left my lips, the answer crashed into my head. My God, the reason why Ibrahim wasn't at the school was blindingly simple. Three years had passed. He was now too old, beyond the age range the Djibouti government had applied to the school.

Ibrahim was physically clinging to my leg, the smile going at full throttle. Through the interpreter, we explained to the tribal chief that this was the child who had inspired me to build the school at As Eyla. The child whose dream of an education was the passion of his young life.

The tribal leader was a man of fairly few words but plenty of action. Pretty much ignoring the old woman, he picked up Ibrahim and dumped him in the car. We all drove to the school, Ibrahim's arms still wrapped around my neck. At the school, an exception was agreed, and one of the new polo shirts was found and pulled down over his head.

Ibrahim was taken to a classroom and put at a desk. By now, the smile was off the scale. Job done.

•   •   •

The twelve footballs and the cones to mark out a pitch, those items that had cost me so dearly at airport customs, were soon in use in the school at As Eyla. The international language of football meant that there were no communication problems between me and the boys. Football had been my passion as a teenager. I'd had some genuine talent; I'd even had trials for a few football league clubs and briefly saw the dazzling chance of a professional career, but I'd screwed it up by not applying myself with the discipline that was needed. Just like the gift of my education, my talent at football was something I'd treated carelessly and thrown away. Another one of life's hard lessons.

But the first match I played with the boys in Djibouti was significant in more ways than one. Far away, back in my home town of Blackpool, a tragedy had just taken place. A young lad called Jordan Banks, aged only nine, had died after being struck by lightning while playing football. Jordan was a kid with an angelic face and a warm, loving nature. He was a little dynamo who had raised money for local charities and got to know some of his neighbourhood police officers, sometimes leaving packets of Haribo sweets on the bonnets of their cars just to cheer them up. With a generosity of heart like that, who knows what Jordan Banks might have gone on to achieve in his life. I was deeply sad because his parents were friends of mine and, naturally, a Blackpool boy named Jordan had a special resonance. There is nothing sadder than a young life cut short, a seedling cut down. Through the interpreter, I told the boys at As Eyla that I wanted to dedicate our game to Jordan's memory. I didn't want to upset them or make them scared that a bolt of lightning might strike them down too, so I phrased it carefully and just trusted that my meaning translated well: that every moment of life is precious and shouldn't be wasted. I explained to them that in my country we often remembered those who had died by bowing our heads and staying silent for one minute – even at a football match. They were fascinated by this concept, one quite alien to them, but they did it perfectly. We also wrote out his name with stones on the sand, along with the number seven, which had been the number on Jordan's football shirt. And so, we played our game in memory of Jordan from Blackpool. It wasn't much, but it was something.

I really hoped that all the boys on the pitch that day, despite the deprivations of their childhood, would seize every opportunity that might come their way to grasp their own personal potential. The potential that had been so evident in young Jordan Banks and so suddenly and cruelly taken away. This school was perhaps the first of those opportunities; I hoped that every one of them would grasp it and one day far in the future look back and acknowledge it as such. If that happened, I'd be a happy man.

• • •

When I returned to the city, I finally met the Minister of Education again, that guy into whose office I'd once walked in a T-shirt and flip-flops. Today, I made sure I was smart. The minister hadn't been at the opening ceremony, but he'd gone out to see the school as soon as possible, making sure it was fit for purpose and that funds would be allocated to pay for the teachers, desks, chairs and so on. That early visit was important because it meant the Djibouti government had taken firm control of the school before any of the conflicting local tribal leaders might try to do the same. As a government school, it would be subject to stringent controls: audits, inspections and above all adherence to the United Nations Sustainability Goals, one of which states that equality of education is a human right. Had I just handed over the school to the local tribal leaders, these criteria might possibly have been watered down with nepotism and places being found for their own children, nieces and nephews, children of friends and so on. Being a government school would put a stop to such practices.

'You kept your promise,' the minister said now. 'Thank you.'

'I always keep my promises,' I replied.

'Most people don't, even if they mean well. But you did it. Djibouti is grateful to you.'

Now that he trusted me, he seemed to hope that I might contribute more to Djibouti in the future. He outlined some distressing scenarios that the country was trying its best to address. One of these was the tragic fact that 95 per cent of children who are blind or deaf have zero hope of any education whatsoever. Their families are often embarrassed, ashamed of their disabilities and keep them hidden away. Nor were there support facilities for disabled children or any people trained to help them. Not one person in the whole of Djibouti was able to teach sign language. The minister asked if I knew of any British volunteers who might go out and teach these skills (and hopefully a few such teachers will be going out to Africa later this year). Once again, there was that shameful old comparison with the prosperous countries of the West and the reminder of how much we all take for granted.

Till this meeting, I'd not really grasped how much political sensitivity was caught up in the opening of the school. The minister had been upset about one report in a British newspaper which had said that without this school these children would never have any education and would remain illiterate for the rest of their lives. And though that was indeed possible, it wasn't an absolute certainty. From the minister's point of view, such a statement made him look bad at his job, which in a country with many challenges was far from fair. I made a note to try to make sure future press coverage of the Great British Paddle didn't contain negative comments like that. Djibouti is a fine country, an oasis in a sea of conflicts, full of good people like the minister trying to do their very best.

One of my worries was what would happen to the kids at the school after their time there was finished and they were ready to move on. Would there be anywhere for them to move on to? Hopefully, my chum the minister would do his utmost to make sure that didn't happen, and I knew that NGOs such as UNICEF were already aware of the issue and working on answers. How sad, cruel even, it would be if at the age of seven or eight and having been given a firm educational foundation, their schooling ground to a screeching halt.

But my trip to As Eyla wasn't just so I could be patted on the back; it had one further purpose which I believed would be really important for the future. As I wrote earlier in this book, almost as soon as I had the idea of building a school, I also had the notion of one day bringing parties of Army Cadets and other groups of British kids out to see the finished school, to observe how people live in cultures so very distant from their own. I hoped that they might see what a difference they might one day be able to make to the lives of people born in less fortunate circumstances and that it would make them appreciate their own advantages. And perhaps above all, I wanted to introduce them to the wider world, the world beyond their bedrooms where they sat glued to their computers and their phones, their connections with others so hugely reliant on technology. I wanted to drag them away from all that for a while. I wanted to get their bums off their chairs and onto bumpy roads with potholes, to get their eyes off their screens to look at infinitely wider horizons.

So, I used some of my time in Djibouti to research the possibilities and logistics of this plan, talking to the tribal leaders, the teachers and others who might be interested in that project. I envisaged taking about a dozen teenagers every year, their costs sponsored by various UK companies who had been supportive to me in the past. I devised a potential seven-day programme of activities for the British kids, including 'social impact' work such as helping to build a better playground for the school or a football pitch or a library for the village, or getting involved in a water sanitation project for the area. They'd be shown life in the desert and go camel trekking or to work at the nearby sanctuary for cheetahs and other wildlife. In short, it would be a unique, once-in-a-lifetime educational opportunity. Selfishly, it would also be a way of keeping my connection to the school alive and relevant in the years to come. I certainly didn't want to become just some bloke who pitched up now and again and for the kids to say to each other, 'Look out, that old guy's back again.' I hoped for a legacy that would have some real meaning beyond just a name on a plaque, and that I might be something more to them than some nutter who once paddled out to sea on a glorified plank.

•   •   •

In As Eyla, little Ibrahim is now at his desk with his pens and pencils and colouring books. I like to believe that the education he so longed for is everything he hoped it would be and more, so the feeling takes root inside him that with hard work and a dash of good luck he can make himself into whoever he wants to be.

Hopefully too, he's getting that weekly English lesson – and maybe I'll start learning his language as well – so that sometime, somewhere, he and I might be able to talk to each other without needing to use a translator. In a way, of course, that isn't too important. He and I had managed to communicate on the only level that really mattered: as two human beings from very different worlds, who came together by chance and made something happen. The African boy who dreamed of going to school and the English boy who dreamed of leaving it but realised his mistake before it was too late. Hopefully, we both learnt something from each other. I'm pretty sure we did.

AFTERWORD

'Be the difference that makes a difference.'

In 2021, almost a year after my Great British Paddle expedition, Brendon Prince wrote history as he became the first person to circumnavigate mainland Great Britain on a stand-up paddleboard, establishing at the same time the longest ever paddleboard journey, surpassing my efforts by more than 1,000km – incredible stuff, congratulations, buddy! I always knew it wouldn't be long before somebody else achieved the goal I'd been prevented from reaching myself, and I'm totally delighted that it was Brendon. A very inspiring adventurer and a genuine, lovely man with a big heart – the latter fact proven by his great generosity in writing the foreword to this book. It was privilege to be asked to be an ambassador for Brendon's expedition, aptly named 'The Long Paddle 2021', and I wish him all the success in the world on his mission to raise awareness of the importance of water safety for young people globally.

For my part, I will continue my mission to try to inspire young people around the world through the spirit of adventure and access to education. And in the meantime, I am preparing to finish my polar marathons in 2022 with expeditions scheduled to the North Pole and Antarctica. The next adventure awaits...

Jordan Wylie
November 2021

ABOUT THE AUTHOR

© *James May Media*

Jordan Wylie is a bestselling author, extreme adventurer and charity fundraiser. He is one of the stars of Channel 4's award-winning and BAFTA-nominated *Hunted* and *Celebrity Hunted*, and he appears regularly on platforms such as Sky News, the BBC and ITV. He is the United Kingdom's national ambassador for the Army Cadet Force, in which capacity he is a frequent motivational speaker to young people in schools and colleges, as well as to businesses all over the world. Jordan is also a multiple Guinness World Record holder and the author of *Citadel* (Mirror Books, 2017), which details his life experiences from a council estate in Blackpool to the battlefield and beyond, and *Running For My Life* (Biteback, 2019), which illustrates how he ran through the most dangerous countries in the world to help inspire children.